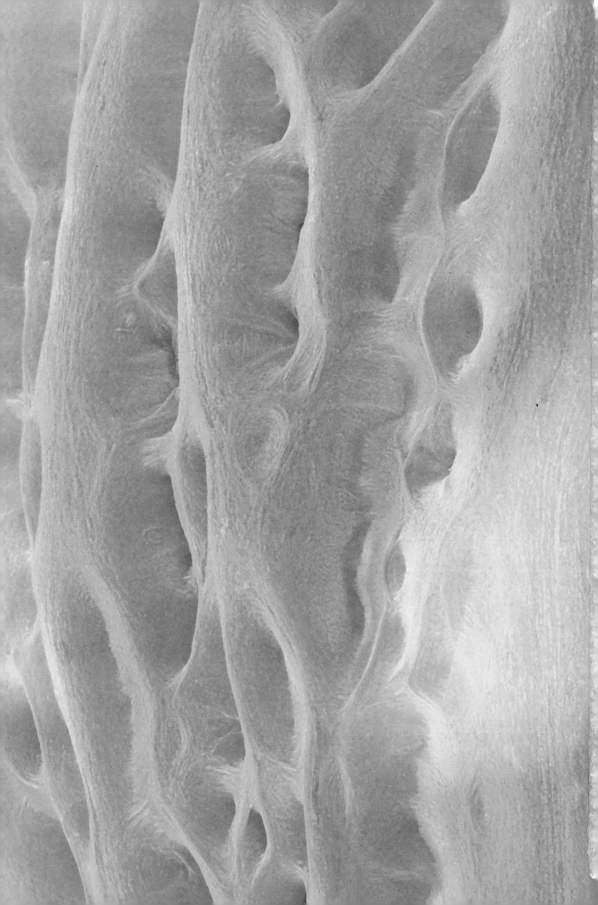

CACAO

DOMINIQUE PERSOONE   EXPEDITION IN MEXICO

CACAO

DOMINIQUE PERSOONE   **EXPEDITION IN MEXICO**

The Roots of Chocolate
as told to Jean-Pierre Gabriel

FRANÇOISE BLOUARD

Foreword

It was the beginning of 2007, and for the first time I was driving through the Mexican jungle at the wheel of a jeep, with two companions, Eddy and Jacky. We were looking for the true wild cocoa, the criollo of Central America. At the time, I could not imagine that, 18 months later, a book would appear about my love for this wonderful country, and about cocoa and its secrets.

By the time I returned home, I was so impressed by everything I had seen and learned that I dreamed of sharing this experience with my fellow chocolate makers and all lovers of chocolate.

I had to go back, and I did so a year later.

This project could never have taken shape without Eddy Van Belle, the creator of Choco-Story, the museum of chocolate. Eddy put into preparing this expedition all his knowledge, all his passion for Latin America and for the history of civilizations (and cocoa ...) and all his energy.

Nor could it have come to fruition without the invaluable help of Mathieu Brees, my friend and fellow Belgian chocolate maker who lives in Mérida. Mathieu was our mentor on the journey into the world of cocoa which led to this book.

A man who kept a good head at all times, who always made me laugh even in the tensest, most frightening moments of our adventure, a fan of high-tech, an engineer at heart, a generous spirit, Agustin Otegui Galindo is the best guide in Mexico!

The most difficult thing was to find someone who would be able to transpose this expedition into a written narrative. This person had to be on the same wavelength as me, as well as being a fantastic writer, a first-class photographer and, ideally, a true gourmet! Because spending long hours on the road seems less long when you talk about food.

With Jean-Pierre Gabriel, I hit it off immediately. I knew I was going to collaborate with someone who lives for his subject – and who in addition is the most discriminating gourmet I know – it was almost too good to be true...

Back in Bruges, I had to come down off the clouds and run my shop. That cannot be done without a great team. To all my colleagues at The Chocolate Line, thank you!

Another team joined us to produce the work you have in your hands. I am thinking particularly of Jurgen Persijn, who conceived the graphic layout, as well as the translators and proofreaders who, each in his or her own way, enriched our words.

Rik Balcaen did not take part in this journey. But from the outset, he has helped me to make my dreams a reality, both personally and on behalf of Belcolade.

Last but not least, if my dear wife Fabienne and my son Julius had not given me the freedom to do the things I live for and indulge my passion, my love for chocolate, this book would never have seen the light of day.

Fabby, Julius, thanks!

DOMINIQUE PERSOONE

Contents

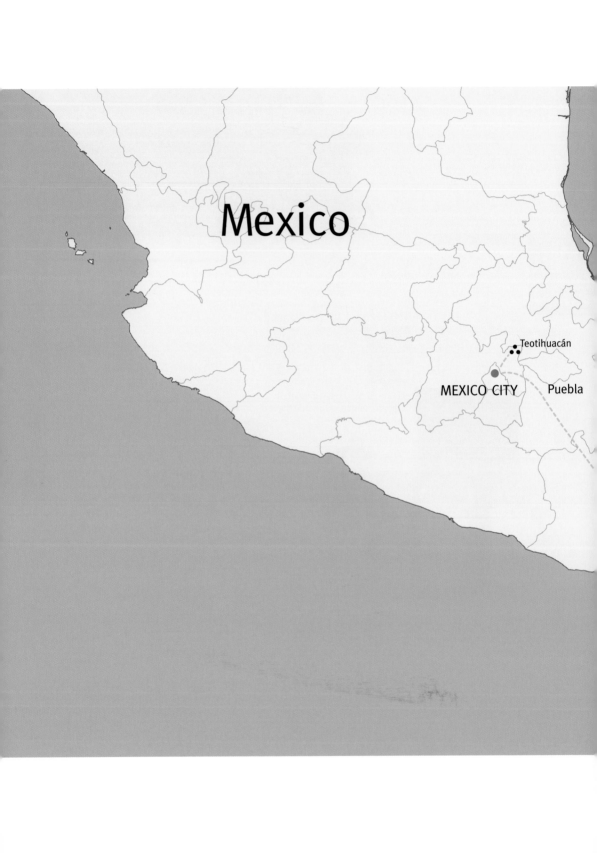

Seeds, money and gods

"Por metaphora se decia del cacao, que solamente lo usaban beber los señores senadores valientes, hombres nobles y generosos ; porque valia mucho y habiamuy poco."

Bernardino de Sahagún, ± 1550

With 150,000 inhabitants at its height, Teotihuacán (opposite, the Avenue of the Dead and the Temple of the Moon; following page, aerial view of part of the city) had a major influence on the whole of Mayan civilization. Traces can be found at Yaxchilán (below, a stele dedicated to one of the kings of the Jaguar Bird dynasty).

It was not yet seven in the morning when we reached Teotihuacán. Our car was third in line and we waited patiently for the gates to open. The official opening time having already passed, we asked the attendant the reason for the delay. He apologized and explained that he was having to count the previous day's takings again.

That one of the most visited, and certainly one of the most impressive, sites in the world should hang in suspense while an employee cross-checked something struck me as quite delightful.

We finally entered the site, and were the first to head for the pyramids. Two stray dogs walked with us. As the morning was still cool, we had no difficulty climbing the Pyramid of the Sun.

For several long minutes, we were alone at the top of the pyramid, surveying the surrounding countryside over an area of several kilometres. Below us, the Avenue of the Dead led towards the Pyramid of the Moon. For a moment, past and future merged, and you only had to close your eyes to hear the sounds of ancient times.

Given its climate and latitude, there are no cocoa trees in Teotihuacán. But this visit was not irrelevant. At its height, in about 500 AD, in other words, bang in the middle of the classic period, this great cosmopolitan metropolis had more than 150,000 inhabitants, among whom were foreigners from Veracruz, Oaxaca or the region of the Mayas, each group living in its own neighbourhood.

Teotihuacán was not isolated on its plain, as it may seem to be today, fifty kilometres north of Mexico City. On the contrary, it had an unequalled influence on the whole of the Mesoamerican sub-continent, from the north of Yucatán to the Pacific coast of Guatemala – the extent of the Mayan world at the time.

It has been demonstrated that the organizational model and, even more, the values of Teotihuacán permeated the political and religious ideas of the Mayas. This influence can also be felt in Mayan art, and even in the glyphs used in their writing. To give only one example, a city as distant as Yaxchilán, situated in the jungle on the banks of the river Usumacinta, contains a bas-relief depicting figures from Teotihuacán, such as Queen K'ahal Xook.

What does all this mean? Quite simply that we should not confine ourselves to a sequential idea of the Central America of that period. The dominance of one civilization, one ethnic group, did not always mean the disappearance of the traditions and customs of a subject people. The era of the Mexicas is a case in point. It is known, for example, that the *pochteca*, the caste of long-distance merchants, spoke a language from the region of Chontalpa, which means that they were Mayas from what is now the state of Tabasco, not far from Veracruz. And the *pochteca* were responsible, among other things, for the transportation of the cocoa paid as tax by the prosperous province of Soconusco, on the Pacific coast of Chiapas.

It was in this context that the world and legend of cocoa developed. These words are not chosen at random. Cocoa was indeed a kind of religion: after all, the Aztecs reserved it for their ruling classes and for the worship of their gods. In his *Apologética historia sumaria*, Bartolomé de las Casas, a Spanish Dominican who was bishop of Chiapas towards the middle

of the 16th century, describes ceremonies that took place three times a year, in which offerings were made to the gods of tempting dishes of poultry and other meats and "as a drink, cocoa completely covered in *espuma*, the finest, that which is drunk by the worthies."

By the time the conquistadors reached their New Spain at the beginning of the 16th century, cocoa was being consumed as a drink – and only as a drink – throughout Central America. We may even consider it a link between peoples, from the north of Mexico to Nicaragua, simply because it was a currency that everyone recognized.

Despite the differences of language, and the recurring hostilities between ethnic groups, there was a genuine community based on cocoa and chocolate, one which endured for centuries and which found expression in the way they were consumed, in the containers used to serve them and the decorations on these containers, and in the rituals and legends which grew up around them.

The preparation of cocoa, although it may involve a varied range of condiments, always follows the same pattern. The beans are first washed and dried. Then they are roasted and, once their husks are removed, ground.

They are then blended into a drink, sometimes containing corn, and combined with spices, from pepper to vanilla, from annatto to *zapote*, or even dried flowers, which give it an aniseed taste. Depending on the region and the circumstances, this drink, sweetened with honey, may be consumed hot or cold.

When it is taken up by the élite, the drink is adulterated in such a way as to

produce froth. It would be interesting to know the rules of this "chocolate ceremony" and the way it developed over the centuries.

It is time to ask *the* existential question, the question which should niggle at us every time we bite into a bar of chocolate.

What is the basis of this addiction, which in some people can become an obsession?

The answer is rather dully molecular. Chemistry and neurophysiology teach us that the cocoa component of chocolate contains powerful psychoactive compounds, such as methylxanthines (caffeine and theobromine), amphetamines, cannabinoids and flavonoids – the last of these having, moreover, the power

Previous pages: the Templo del Sol at Teotihuacán. Above, the Templo del Sur at Yaxchilán. Following pages: the *ceiba*, the mythical tree of the Mayas. More than forty metres high, it symbolizes the union of the underworld and the heavens.

to reduce high levels of cholesterol.

With all these mysteries only partly solved, it is time to go back to the source: the tropical rain forest. It is here, in the translucent shade of other, larger trees, that the cocoa tree grows. The freshly gathered pod is opened, releasing a delicious white pulp in which the seeds are loosely confined. The bitterness of these seeds makes it difficult to eat them as they are, so a way must be found to make them more pleasant to the palate.

We could be in one of the managed forests of what will become the province of Soconusco, in Chiapas, on the border between Mexico and Guatemala, in an orchard of *criollo* cocoa trees.

In 1825, the French gastronome Jean Anthelme Brillat-Savarin wrote in his *Physiologie du goût*: "The cocoa tree is native to southern America (...) It is agreed now that the trees which give the best fruit are those which grow on the banks of the Maracaïbo, in the valleys of Caracas and in the rich province of Sokomusco."

The tree
and its fruits

"Esta fruta nace dentro de unas masorca,
en árboles muy frescos : esto se llama cacauatl ;
pero como los españoles como toda esta tierra
han corrompido la lengua, y lo llaman cacao ;
de esto hay mucho en este rio arriba..."

Tomás de la Torre, 1544

Opposite, an orchard of cocoa trees, from the Azoyú Codex, an illustrated book compiled in about 1565. Above, a pod from a wild cocoa tree. Its shape suggests that it is a *criollo*.

It was in 1753 that the word *cacao*, borrowed from the Mayan language, was recognized by science. In that year, the famous Swedish naturalist Carl Linnaeus undertook a true labour of Hercules, bringing order to the classification of the vegetable kingdom by giving each "plant" two linked names, their order determined by a strict hierarchy. So, for example, the cocoa tree was given the binomial *Theobroma cacao*.

Since Linneaus assumed that there were other plants, other trees, similar to the cocoa tree, he decided that cocoa was a species, which he included within a larger unit, a genus. To find a suitable name, he drew on the reputation which cocoa beans had acquired in Central America of being the food (*broma*) of the gods (*theo*).

According to the latest authoritative publications, the genus *Theobroma* includes some twenty species of tree, including, among others, *Theobroma bicolor*, known in Central America by the vernacular name *pataxte*.

Of the *Theobroma* trees, the cocoa tree may grow to an adult height of between 12 and 15 metres in its natural state. I had the opportunity to see such slender specimens in Yucatán, in the *cenote* of Aktun Sitio, which I will describe later in this book.

When cultivated, the available space being more restricted, they reach a lesser height, varying from 4 to 8 metres. Such is the case, for example, at La Joya, where the Echeverría family has developed a very functional system of cultivation, controlling even the height to which the trees can grow.

The different species of the genus *Theobroma* bear a family resemblance. One of

Heart-shaped pods of a *cundeamor* cocoa, »
a type of *forastero*.

Opposite, a *calabacillo* cocoa in full bloom. Above, the white cotyledons: the colour is the unmistakable mark of a *criollo* cocoa, here a *blanco marfil*.

their characteristics is the way the flowers grow in clumps directly on the trunk. These small, delicate flowers are produced in their thousands – some 20,000 per tree per year – but give birth to only a few dozen fruits.

These fruits, the pods, become coloured when they ripen, after a process of maturation which lasts between 5 and 6 months from the pollination of the flower.

Anyone attempting to become familiar with the language of cocoa needs to learn a specific vocabulary.

At the basic level, we find three types of cocoa tree: *criollo, forastero* and *trinitario*. In the next chapter, we shall see how the last of these was born out of the encounter between the first two, which originally grew separately in nature. In other words, the terms *criollo* and *forastero* refer to wild plants, whereas *trinitario* designates a hybrid produced by human intervention.

Generally speaking, a cocoa tree of the *forastero* type is more robust and more resistant to disease than its *criollo* counterpart, and therefore gives a greater yield. There is little variation among the pods of a *criollo* cocoa tree. They have a regular elliptical shape, ending in a point. They are usually green, turning yellow or red when they ripen.

Among the pods of *forasteros* and *trinitarios*, on the other hand, there is great disparity. In 1882, the botanist Sir Daniel Morris paved the way for a classification of "*cacaos*". He first distinguished the *criollos* and the *forasteros*. Then, on the basis of the morphology of the pod, he divided *forasteros* into several types: *cundeamor, amelonado, calabacillo*, and so on.

These words, which refer to shapes – a heart, a melon, a calabash – are still used today. *Trinitarios*, which, being hybrids, theoretically have characteristics of both

Cacao cundeamor

Cacao amelonado

Above, a newly opened cocoa pod, with a mixture of white (*criollo*) and mauve (*forastero* or *trinitario*) seeds, a sign of cross-pollination. Opposite, the purplish colour of the inside of the seed indicates that this cocoa is not a *criollo*, but a *forastero* or *trinitario*.

their parents, can also be classified in this way.

All pods, whatever their origin, shape and colour, are similarly structured. This becomes evident when we cut a pod in half widthwise. Each circular section reveals, beneath the coloured skin, a hard white part, known as the pericarp or cortex.

In its centre, the seeds – between 25 and 75 in each pod, with the average being about 40 – are distributed in five cavities arranged in the shape of a star. They are surrounded by a delicious, sweet-smelling mucilaginous pulp. If all the seeds in a pod are round, and their flesh is white or slightly pink, we can be certain we are

dealing with a *criollo* cocoa tree. The seeds of a *forastero* or a *trinitario* are flatter in shape, and their insides – whether in a fresh or dried state – are crimson.

The seeds and the pulp are both edible. In the days when hunter-gatherers were attempting to appropriate the products of the wild flora around them, the first "cocoa lovers" were no doubt attracted by the sweetness of the pulp. They then also became aware that the beans produced a tonic effect on them, just like other plants growing wild in the forest, such as cola.

Three thousand years later, these properties still draw us. Time and technology have done the rest.

The jungle of species

"*The Mesoamerican trees were distinguished by long, pointed, warty, soft, and deeply ridged pods which contained seeds with white cotyledons; while the South American ones had hard, round, melon-like pods, and the seeds had purplish cotyledons.*"

Sophie D. Coe, Michael D. Coe, *The True History of Chocolate*, 1996

Opposite, typical landscapes of Chiapas, one of the cocoa-producing regions of Mexico. Above, like all *Theobromas*, the cocoa tree bears its fruits on its trunk and large branches.

Criollo, Forastero, Trinitario. For the chocolate expert, these words are part of everyday language. They correspond to the three great types of cocoa tree cultivated. Originally, two of them grew in nature. The differences between them have been recognized and accepted, since they do not bear the same names in the official botanical classification.

Theobroma cacao ssp cacao designates a 'wild' sub-species, that is, *cacao criollo*, and *Theobroma cacao ssp shaerocarpum* is the name of another naturally occurring sub-species, *cacao forastero*. In botanical jargon, the word *cacao* refers to a species and the word *Theobroma* to a genus. As for the abbreviation *ssp*, it indicates that we are dealing with a sub-species.

Strictly speaking, it is barely possible to use the singular here, given the large number of varieties of *cacao criollo* and *cacao forastero*.

Let us imagine that you are in a plantation. How to distinguish a *forastero* from a *criollo*? A botanist can apply organic criteria, such as the appearance and colour of the pods, how hard their skin is, whether the seeds are round or flat, the colour of the sterile stamens, and so on.

The layman, though, has one infallible test: the colour of the cotyledons which make up the bulk of the seed. Cutting one of the seeds in half, we see that the cotyledons, which are the main part of its "flesh", are clearly purple in a *forastero* and between milky white and slightly pink in a *criollo*.

If the above does not apply to them, and if they are not defined as "wild", what, then, are the cocoa trees known as *trinitarios*? To understand their origin, try to imagine a garden. In this garden, two cocoa trees foreign to one another, a *criollo* and a *forastero*, are brought together. When the trees flower, the insects do their work and, in carrying pollen from the flowers of one tree to those of its neighbour, bring about a crossing of the two trees, that is, the two sub-species. The fruits of this cross-fertilization bear seeds. When these are sown, hybrid plants are born, which become cocoa trees inheriting the characteristics of both their originally very different parents.

This adventure in the plant world took place during the 18th century on the island of Trinidad. There are few written texts to

A cocoa tree produces between ten and twenty thousand flowers per year, of which only a few dozen become pods. Following pages: the tree nursery on the *hacienda* Jesús Maria uses cocoa clones that can withstand disease.

tell us exactly what happened, but Sophie and Michael D. Coe have tried to chart it in their work *The True History of Chocolate*, one of my bedside books.

Discovered by Christopher Columbus, Trinidad is a large island situated close to the mouth of the Orinoco. When the Spanish arrived, they first set about exterminating the indigenous population. Subsequently, Capuchin friars from Catalonia and Aragon established missions there. It was probably these friars who first brought *criollo* cocoa seeds with them in 1525. Cocoa trees were grown on the island until 1727. That year, a cataclysm of unknown origin – it may have been a storm, it may have been some kind of plant epidemic – destroyed the plantations. Two or three decades later, the Capuchins resumed cocoa cultivation on the island of Trinidad, importing trees from Venezuela, probably from the Orinoco delta.

Scientists do not agree on the genetic profile of the imported trees. Some argue that they were *forasteros* and that it was then that the marriage took place between the newcomers and *criollos* which had grown again spontaneously, long after the disaster of 1727.

CACAO CLONAL
TIPO CRIOLLO
ALMENDRA
RUBIA

Others think it more likely that the union between *criollos* and *forasteros* had already been effected previously, on some of the small islands in the Orinoco delta, and that the Capuchins simply replanted trees which were already *trinitarios* before they even arrived in Trinidad.

At this point, it is worth examining the etymology of the words *criollo* and *forastero*, as applied to types of cocoa tree. The first, which means creole, should be understood in the sense of 'typical'. As for the second, it designates, in contrast, a stranger in a region or a place.

All of which begs the question, concerning these two types: which is typical, and in relation to which place? The answer can be found in Venezuela. It would appear that the first cocoa tree grown in that country was of the *criollo* type. *Forastero* trees were planted later, brought in from their region of origin.

A further Pandora's box opens up when we consider a question which remains unresolved to this day: the journey which cocoa made before it was cultivated and before Central America established its reputation and raised its fruit to the status of drink of the gods.

It is now accepted that the original habitat of the genus *Theobroma* was the tropical rainforest. The species of the genus *Theobroma*, and those of one of its closest relatives, the genus *Herrania*, are native to the basins of the Amazon and the Orinoco, as well as their tributaries. Some researchers have gone further and contended that the species *cacao* has its origin in a specific area situated not far from the border between Colombia and Ecuador, east of the foothills of the Andes.

This means that, somewhere in this forest, the two sub-species – *criollo* and *forastero* – grew without ever coming into contact. More than 2,000 years ago, the *criollo* moved north, while the *forastero* migrated southwards. And it was not until the colonial period that, at the instigation of man, the two sub-species were finally brought into contact and cross-fertilized one another.

Based on what we now know, it would seem that their destinies were very different. The *forastero* probably evolved in societies which were socially and technically less developed. It is quite likely that, for centuries, it was adapted by man for human consumption only in a fairly rudimentary way, typical of the early hunter-gatherers.

It seems, in fact, to have become clear to man from an early period that the pods of the *Theobroma* and the *Herrania* contained seeds and a pulp which were not only not poisonous but actually edible. What was more, these by-products both provided two nutritional elements spontaneously sought by the human body: a sweetener – mainly located in the pulp – and a stimulant, owing, among other things, to the theobromine and caffeine in the seeds.

It has been established that, throughout the pre-Columbian period, the uses to which these products were put differed greatly in South America and Central America, including Mexico.

This difference in the use of elements extracted from the *Herrania* pod and, especially, the *Theobroma* pod is still in evidence today. In the north, on the one hand, "chocolate" obtained from beans – whether fermented or not – which are

Man first consumed the fruits of the cocoa tree in the form of a beverage, obtained by dipping the pulp and seeds **»** in water. Following pages: pods from a "wild" cocoa tree in the Lacandon jungle.

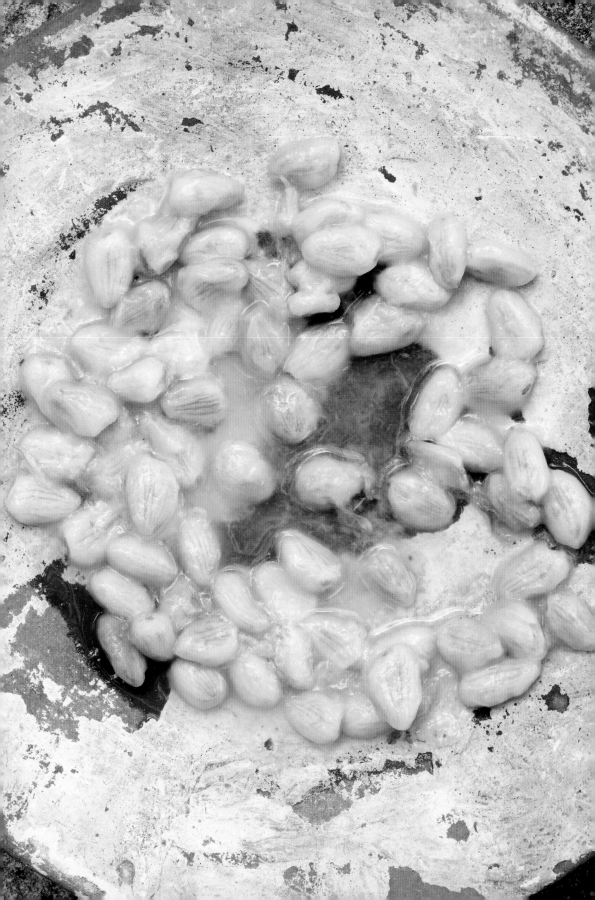

dried, then roasted, is a national drink in Mexico. On the other hand, drinks made from cocoa pulp are widely sold in Brazil, and are even available in cans and cartons or – a real sign of the times – in frozen form.

Similarly, from Bolivia to Venezuela, cocoa pulp is fermented in order to make products as disparate as alcoholic drinks and vinegar.

To obtain an even fuller picture, we also need to take a brief look at *Theobroma bicolor*. This is quite a large tree often found in gardens and plantations in Mexico, particularly in areas where the Mayan influence is still felt. The *pataxte*, as it is called in Central America, is also known as *balamte*, a more poetic word, meaning 'the jaguar tree', in reference to the wonderful texture the skin of the pods develops when it dries.

Less sweet than the pulp of *Theobroma cacao*, the pulp of *Theobroma bicolor* is still consumed as a drink in some regions.

In popular imagery, this pulp was seen as a viaticum for the dead as they started out on their long journey to the other world. Moreover, among the Mayas, *pataxte* beans had, until the beginning of the 20th century, the same monetary value as cocoa beans.

But to return to the legendary and still mysterious odyssey of the first *cacaos* – *criollos* – from their region of origin to the furthest end of their area of acclimatization, that is, the region of Chichén Itzá, in the state of Yucatán: this migration, which presupposes a crossing of the isthmus of Panama, is still the subject of much speculation, and there are several convergent but slightly different theories.

How did these early civilizations manage to bring such perishable pods hundreds and hundreds of kilometres through tropical jungle? That is a question for which there is as yet no answer.

Everything, however, points to there having been a route going along the Pacific coast – which would argue in favour of the idea that cocoa first arrived in the region of Soconusco, in the southwest of what is now the state of Chiapas. Further east, it established itself in the region of Tabasco and in the Lacandon jungle. Several studies have claimed that this jungle still contains *criollo* cocoa trees which are the descendants of the first trees grown from natural seedlings.

The writings of Spanish travellers in the 16th century describe the "orchards" of cocoa trees as managed forests. In other words, the trees were clearly grown in an environment similar to their original habitat. The ecological – and spiritual – approach clearly prevailed over the need for intensive agriculture.

The centuries from the first attempts at domesticating the cocoa tree to the transformation of its seeds into a drink for the elite to their adoption as currency were among the most exciting in the epic of cocoa.

« In traditional gardens, *Theobroma bicolor* or *pataxte* can still be found. The skin of its fruit has earned it the name "jaguar tree".

A bean
that counts

*"I remarked, what I had heard of,
but had not seen before, that grains of cacao
circulated among the Indians as money."*

John Lloyd Stephens, *Incidents of Travel in Yucatán*, 1843

A suffering Christ from the 16th century, in the San José chapel of the cathedral in Mexico City. People still make offerings to it in the form of cocoa beans. Until early in the 20th century, cocoa beans were used as currency in some states of Mexico.

Two very different images come to mind. The first can be found at the entrance to the museum at the archaeological site of Tonina. It is a beautiful ceramic figure of a monkey wearing a necklace made mostly of cocoa pods.

The other can be found in the cathedral in Mexico City, built by the Catholic Church beside the ruins of the great Aztec edifice, the Templo Mayor.

Entering by the left door, we see a chapel dedicated to San José, with a baroque altarpiece. Pilgrims hurrying through will miss a magnificent *Ecce homo* tucked away in this chapel. It is a seated polychrome statue of the suffering Christ, made from stalks of corn and called *El Señor del cacao*.

Dating from the 16th century, this figure was greatly venerated by the indigenous people at the time of colonization. As an offering, they would place cocoa beans before it. There is a probably spurious legend claiming that the accumulated value of these beans financed the building of the cathedral, which was completed in 1667.

According to the writings of Brother Thomas Gage from the beginning of the 17th century, the comfort in which the monks lived at that time was due to the gifts of cocoa beans left before the images of Christ and the saints.

The monkey at Tonina has a more naturalistic significance. There are in fact a number of bas-reliefs from the end of the classic period (c.700 to 900 AD) which show a spider monkey and a cocoa pod. Although the latter is used as a decorative element, the monkey is often shown carrying a pod or with a pod hanging from the end of its tail.

In the museum at Tonina, a magnificent ceramic of a monkey's head wearing a necklace of cocoa pods.

Some have concluded that monkeys were sacrificed in rituals. Others point to the fact that, in nature, the monkey is one of the animals that feeds on the fruits of the cocoa tree. Like the squirrel, though, it also spreads the seeds – after they have made their way through its intestinal tract!

There is ample evidence of the role played by Central America in the birth of chocolate, even in the forms in which we know it today, from the cultivation of cocoa trees in the forest to the description of a banquet held by the Emperor Mote-cuhzoma Xocoyotzin, found in the writings of the conquistador Bernal Diáz del Castillo. In his memoirs, Bernal Diáz relates that "fine gold goblets were regularly brought in, containing a certain drink made from cocoa, which is said to help a man seduce a woman!"

It is difficult to give a precise date to the beginning of this extraordinary epic. It may have begun in about 600 BC, or even a few centuries earlier. The first agronomists of the cocoa tree were probably the Olmecs, whose civilization developed in the tropical lowlands south of Veracruz and in what is now the state of Tabasco. The Olmecs have left us remains in the form of colossal heads representing their gods and monarchs, but few other traces have come down to us. There are several reasons for this. The first is the environment in which the cocoa tree grows: the tropical rainforest is not the best place in which to preserve anything. Secondly, Olmec society has left few written texts, although some did appear at the time it was being supplanted by a people who played a major role in the history of cocoa: the Mayas.

Palenque (above) and Uxmal (following pages), two Mayan sites of the classic period.

There have been far more archaeological discoveries relating to the Mayan civilization, from remarkable sites such as Uxmal or Palenque to more modest elements, such as fragments of terra cotta containers. Some of these bear designs in which we can clearly make out a cocoa tree, or its fruits, or even containers used for a drink made from corn or cocoa or both. Scientists have also succeeded in drawing information from these containers. Highly specialised laboratory analyses have revealed residues of caffeine and theobromine. If both elements are present, we may be sure that the container in question contained a liquid food made from cocoa – in this case, a *criollo*. If on the other hand, only theobromine is detected, we know that these are traces of *pataxte*. Unlike *Theobroma cacao*, *Theobroma bicolor* does not contain caffeine.

The later the period we look at, the more information we find. Some sources, though, like Mayan written texts, are cruelly missing, either because they were destroyed in conflicts or, more prosaically, because the medium on which they were written was too fragile to withstand the ravages of time.

We find the same problem of the lack of surviving traces later, when it comes to the illustrated books of the Aztecs (the Mexicas, as they called themselves). Some of this literature from the pre-Colombian era was eliminated following internecine wars, and what remained suffered at the hands of the Inquisition, which was just as virulent in the New World.

These misfortunes make what has survived all the more valuable. Among these survivors is the magnificent Dresden Codex, which dates from just before

the arrival of the Spanish. On one of the pages dealing with new year ceremonies, we can make out, for example, the god Opossum carrying the god of rain on a seat attached to his back. When translated, the glyphs accompanying this illustration read *kakaw u hanal*, which means: *cocoa is food*.

The fact that this type of glyph is used clearly identifies the Dresden Codex – named after the city where it has been kept since 1739 – as a document of Mayan origin. This codex, considered by specialists to be the finest of those which have been preserved, is believed to have been compiled in Chichén Itzá between 1200 and 1250, during what is known as the post-classic period: a time when this part of the world was dominated by the Aztec triple alliance, composed, we may recall, of Tenochtitlán – which is now Mexico City – Texcoco and Tlacopán.

From the above, it may be deduced that both the language and the traditions of the Mayas survived long after they had passed their peak. In the case which concerns us here, this language and its etymology are valuable allies in tracing the social and cultural history of our subject: cocoa.

In other words, to name a thing in a particular language presupposes, for it to be thus named, that this thing has some significance in the society which speaks that language.

The Mayan "word" *kakaw* derives from *kakawa*, which belongs to the vocabulary of an older complex of languages known as Mije-Sokean. Originating in the south of what is now Mexico, Mije-Sokean probably developed about 500 BC, that is, at the end of the Olmec civilization, and

Above, a depiction of Ek Chuah, the god of cocoa, from the Dresden Codex. Opposite, the pigeon house at Uxmal, emerging from the jungle.

subsequently migrated beyond its birthplace, influencing other dialects in a lasting way.

While the expression *kakaw* remained unchanged in the course of Mayan history, the way in which it was written underwent a considerable evolution. In the Dresden Codex – from about 1200 – the glyphs are highly stylised. The same *kakaw* when carved – for example, on

ceramics dating from some five or six centuries earlier – is much more graphic, being made up of full-length anthropomorphic forms, with human heads clearly depicted. It can also be found on a stele in the central arcade of the Templo del Norte in Palenque.

When we decipher this glyph we find something surprising. During the classic period, the head is extended into a fin, meaning *ka* – fish. There are two dots, corresponding to the number two. This gives us *ka-ka*. The remaining sign, beneath the head, is *wa*. As the final *a* is not pronounced in Maya, we end up with *kakaw*...

Many decades later, the term *kakawa*, the root of the word *cacao*, was adopted in Nahuatl – the language spoken by the Aztecs – where it became *kakawa-tl*: the suffix *tl* is a typical phonetic characteristic of Nahuatl, and is found in a large number of common nouns, such as *toma-tl* – tomato.

The question remains as to how *kakawa-tl*, meaning cocoa, led to another Nahuatl word, *chokola:tl*, to identify a drink made from cocoa beans, spices and water.

At this point, it is necessary to put an end to a myth, perhaps forever. Several specialists dispute the Nahuatl origin of the word chocolate. They even claim, with texts to prove it, that the word *chokola:tl* – Hispanicized to *chocolate* – was not part of the Nahuatl language at the beginning of the conquest, that is, about 1520.

Like much of the Nahuatl spoken today, *chokola:tl* was probably the result of a late exchange between Spanish and the

Right, a Mayan glyph in Palenque, representing *ka-ka-w(a)*. The *ka* is symbolized by a fish, whose caudal fin can be made out.

language of the period. In other words, the "European" colonists may have borrowed other words from Nahuatl in order to name a drink which they had already adopted and integrated into their culinary habits.

By way of evidence, we may cite Spanish authors from the late 16th century. In *Relación de Juan Bautista de Pomar* (1582) the author states: "*Su bebida de poderosos era cacao*", which means: "the drink of the powerful is cocoa". We also find several references to the drink cocoa – but not to chocolate! – in the *Historia de las Indias de Nueva España y Islas de Tierra Firme*, written before 1586 by Diego Duran.

Having completed this exploration of the language, and drawn some distressing conclusions, we are still left with many questions.

How did all this come about? Why did these civilizations, which left their mark on world history over some twenty centuries, choose to transform the fruit of the cocoa tree, and to confer on the seeds of that fruit a special status among the products of the edible plants they cultivated?

We must go back to the beginning, that is, to the environment in which wild cocoa grew. It was there, in the tropical rainforest, that the Mayas – and probably the Olmecs before them – chose to grow them. They did not create fields or gardens to which they could transport the plants and cultivate them.

On the contrary, they opted for a kind of forest agriculture. They integrated with the forest and adapted it, in such a way as to create a balance between yield and environment.

This was not an unusual practice: the Mayas used this method to "acclimatize" some 250 types of tree. The chronicles of the first Spanish travellers mention two important "agricultural" regions: Soconusco on the Pacific coast, near the border with Guatemala, and Chontalpa, in the state of Tabasco. Much later, after the year 1000, these same regions were among the main contributors of cocoa beans.

This observation confirms a fascinating fact. The dried seed of the *cacao criollo*, the simple product of a tree which can be reproduced in the tens of thousands, became for centuries both the basis of a highly prized drink, the exclusive preserve of an élite, and a currency in which, for example, solders were paid. As evidence of their value, the storehouses in which these taxes were kept were as heavily guarded as today's bank vaults.

Cocoa beans were genuinely regarded as standard currency. This can be appreciated in the writings of, among others, Toribio de Benavente Motolinia, a Franciscan who was among the first contingent of twelve monks sent to the New World in 1523, as well as one of the founders of the city of Puebla de los Angeles in about 1530.

The first of his peers to learn Nahuatl, this monk was to become a reliable witness of the social and commercial relations in indigenous society. In 1545, for example, he noted that a freshly picked avocado was worth three cocoa beans, that is, the same price as a turkey hen's egg. The turkey hen herself cost 100 beans and the turkey cock 200...

Some three centuries later, in his *Incidents of Travel in Yucatán*, John Lloyd Stephens, a great traveller from New York, witnessed a scene he had never encountered before. "I remarked, what I had heard of, but had not seen before, that cocoa beans circulated among the Indians as money. Each vendor of food – most are women – has on the stall a pile of these beans. They count them constantly and exchange them with the Indians. There are no copper coins in Yucatán (...) and this deficiency is made up for with cocoa beans. (...) This currency still has a real value, which is regulated by the quantity of cocoa on the market."

It was not until 1905 that the governor of Yucatán abolished the use of cocoa beans as currency and replaced them with copper coins.

From the legendary Mendoza Codex, the tributes paid by the province of Soconusco to the Aztec triple alliance. To »» the left of each jaguar skin, the drawing shows a hundred loads of cocoa. Below, two containers totalling 800 *tecamates* and containing a cocoa-based drink.

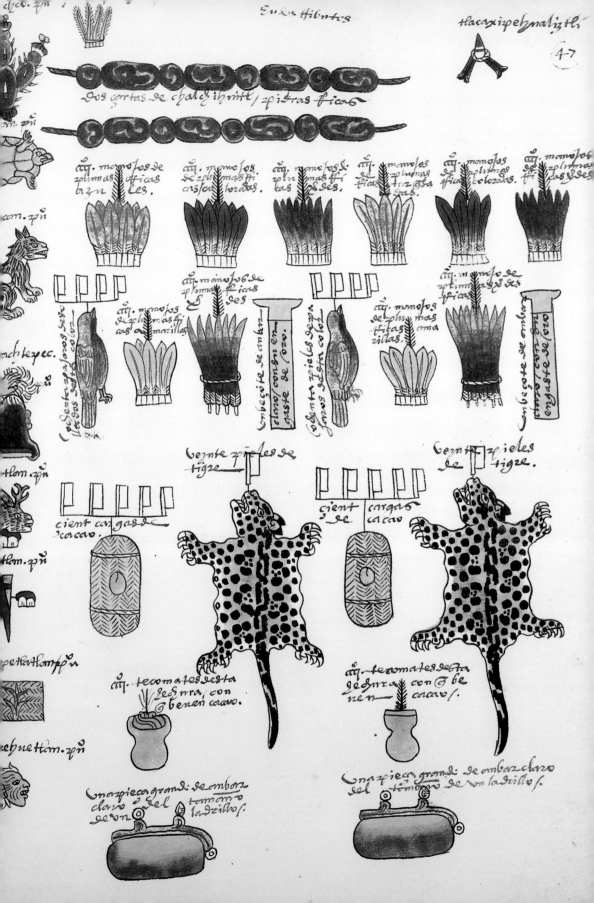

Dos sartas de chalchihuitl / y piedras ficas

cc. manojos de plumas ficas azules

cc. manojos de plumas ficas colorados

cc. manojos de plumas ficas verdes

cc. manojos de plumas ficas berdes

cc. manojos de plumas ficas coloras

cc. manojos de plumas ficas y des

Cosenta paxaros destos destas colores

cc. manojos de plumas ficas amarillas

cc. manojos de plumas ficas verdes

Cabeçita se cobra en guaste de oro

cc. manojos de plumas ficas verdes

cc. manojos de plumas ficas amarillas

Cosenta piezas destos destas colores

Bespeto se cobra en oro con su engaste de oro

Beynte pieles de tigre

Beynte pieles de tigre

cient cargas de cacao

cient cargas de cacao

cc. tecomates desta fechura con que benen cacao.

cc. tecomates desta fechura con que benen cacao.

Una pieça grande de ombar claro del tamaño de un ladrillo.

Una pieça grande de ombar claro del tamaño de un ladrillo.

From field
to seed

"Os frutos amarelos pendiam das árvores como lâmpadas antigas. Maravilhosa mistura de cor que tornava tudo belo e irreal, menos o nosso trabalho estafante."

Jorge Amado, Cacau, 1933

Between opening the pod and obtaining the dried seed, six to ten days may elapse, depending on the type of cocoa: *criollo* or *forastero*.

However abstract it may sometimes seem, history is a fascinating subject. Visiting the ancient Mayan cities, from Chichén Itzá to Palenque, from Uxmal to Yaxchilan, one cannot help but be impressed by the huge size of these complexes. Their imposing character is very appealing, enhanced as it often is by stories handed down by chroniclers of the time. The lack of reliable information – there are many things we still do not know, despite all the efforts of archaeologists and linguists – merely adds to their fascination.

For nearly 2,000 years, from c.500 BC to the arrival of the Spanish, a number of civilizations, from the Olmecs to the Mexicas, contributed to the development of this part of the world, known as Mesoamerica. More than gold or other precious metals, and for reasons which may seem strange, cocoa was one of the major vehicles of this great adventure.

Chontalpa, a sub-region of the state of Tabasco, on the shores of the Gulf of Mexico, is in many respects one of the nerve centres of the cocoa economy. Firstly, the region of Tabasco is, with Soconusco on the Pacific coast, one of the two epicentres where cocoa was domesticated and brought under cultivation in the biotope of the tropical rain forest.

From being a simple product of the earth, the cocoa seed became over the generations a sophisticated ingredient, involved in many aspects of social life. We know for example that the region of Chontalpa traded for a long time with Yucatán, supplying cocoa as currency

Comalcalco, in Chontalpa (state of Tabasco), is a unique example of a site where the buildings are made from terra cotta bricks.

to the merchants of that region.

In the 15th century, the Aztec triple alliance also maintained significant economic relations with this part of Tabasco. The hub during this period, frequently mentioned in the historical sources, was the port of Xicalango, also located in Chontalpa, where the merchants had their storehouses.

It is also in this sub-region that we find a Mayan archaeological site which is unique of its kind: Comalcalco, which dates from the 7th century. What makes it original is the fact that all the buildings are made of baked clay bricks, the raw material for which was obtained locally, and that all these bricks are held together with a mortar made from oyster shells.

And while we are looking at unusual features, it is worth mentioning that the name Comalcalco itself does not come directly from Maya but from Nahuatl, the language spoken, among others, by the Aztecs! *Comalli-calli-co* means the house of *comales*, a *comal* being a slab, originally made of clay, used for baking tortillas – or for roasting cocoa and coffee beans...

I had other reasons for being interested in Comalcalco. The aim of my Mexican expedition was to track down the true *cacao criollo*, to see with my own eyes the trees that bear these pods, to weigh them in my hands, to cut them open with a machete and extract those famous white or slightly pink beans, the unmistakable mark of the *criollo* sub-species.

That was why I had planned a visit to the *hacienda cacaotera* Jesús María, owned by Vicente Gutiérrez Cacep. What made me all the more impatient to stroll among the cocoa trees is that Vicente's father, Teófilo Cacep, is considered to have been one of the pioneer modernizers of cocoa cultivation in Tabasco.

A walk at dawn in the plantation got me off to a promising start. Before the gatherers had even arrived, I spotted a magnificent specimen of *Ceiba pentandra*, the mythical tree of the Mayas. All the treatises on growing cocoa say that young cocoa trees need coolness and shade, provided by taller trees. Reaching a height of at least 40 metres, this *ceiba* was almost certainly just what the doctor ordered ...

My first look around was fascinating. Hanging on the trees and their branches were pods of many colours: bright red, yellow, orange, green. And there was a similar variation on the skin of the pods themselves, the tops of the ribs often having a more intense colour than the hollows between them.

A closer examination of these fruits soon disillusioned me. Few trees on this model plantation presented the outward signs of the *criollo* for which Tabasco and Chontalpa were once famous. What I did see were pods of the *cundeamor*, *calabacillo* and *amelonado* types, which, as we have seen, are categories of *forasteros*, as defined by Morris at the end of the 19th century, and since confirmed by other specialists in plant taxonomy.

But let us return to that rewarding stage: the gathering. Any self-respecting gatherer is equipped with two instruments, both equally sharp. One is the famous machete, which he carries on his belt and keeps with him at all times. The other is a pole at the end of which is a piece of sharpened metal. This *luco*, as it is called, is used for getting ripe pods which are out of reach down from the trunk and the larger branches.

Opposite, a gatherer with his *luco*, a pole fitted with a sickle. Following pages: extracting the pulp and seeds from »
the pod.

Left, sweet cocoa pulp is fermented to reduce bitterness and kill the germ of the seed. Above, an old fermentation vat hollowed out of the trunk of a large American mahogany.

The day's crop is taken to a particular point on the plot of land. It is there that the youngest workers repeat an age-old gesture. Sometimes with a machete, sometimes without, they crack open the husk of the pod and, with their fingers, extract the pulp and the seeds. Usually, these two ingredients are transported together in wooden vats which can hold between 700 kilos and one tonne of fresh materials.

There are more spectacular models of vat. Also in Comalcalco, in the warehouses of the Hacienda de La Luz, I had the opportunity to see a magnificent *toya*: a huge, elongated container more than ten metres long and one metre wide, hollowed out of the trunk of a *caoba*, the American mahogany.

At this point, the process gathers pace, as it is important to take the intrinsic characteristics of the pulp into consideration. Like any fresh, sweet substance placed in an ambient temperature above 25°C, it tends to ferment. It is this ability which is used to chemically transform the fresh seed into a dried bean from which we elaborate the chocolate we know, in Belgium and elsewhere ...

What happens during fermentation?

Firstly, the length of the process varies depending on whether the crop has been gathered from a *criollo* or a *forastero*. Whereas two to three days are sufficient for the fermentation of the former, the latter requires four to six days.

The scenario is similar to any alcoholic fermentation. The yeast present naturally

transforms the sugar to alcohol. This phase is exothermic, in other words it gives off heat. The temperature in a vat can increase by up to 45°C in 48 hours. It is, among other things, to avoid roasting the beans too much that the mass has to be turned over in order to make sure that it is heated as evenly as possible.

Alcoholic fermentation leads to an acidification of the environment, which permits the development of bacteria whose role is to oxidize the alcohol produced into acetic acid. The mixing of the mass is again justified, since it allows for the incorporation of air, and hence oxidation. And it now becomes clear why, in some regions, cocoa pulp is elaborated into an alcoholic drink or into vinegar.

Under the twofold action of acidity and heat, the germs of the seeds are killed, which is one of the specific aims of the fermentation process. Among its other effects, fermentation acts on the reserves of the seed, stored in its cotyledons and half made up of cocoa butter, causing biochemical transformations which reduce the bitterness and develop the aminoacids, as well as simple sugars which give each cocoa its specific flavour.

Once this operation has been completed, there remains another indispensable stage: the drying, which is often done in the open air. For about two days, the seeds are spread on a concrete surface to be warmed by the sun, which can reach a temperature of 40°C during the day.

In a nutshell, the drying brings the fermentation to an end, by blocking the enzymatic reactions. It also decreases the acidity and reduces the water content of the bean to about 7%. Thus "protected", the crop is put into sacks of 62,5 kilos. Add it up: that makes 16 sacks per tonne.

I admit I have no idea when the technique of fermentation was first mastered. We do know that the Mayas, and probably others before them, were familiar with the alcoholic fermentation of sweet materials, without really understanding how it worked. But fermentation does not seem to have been part of the elaboration of cocoa into a "chocolate-flavoured" drink in Mesoamerica, before the Spanish conquest.

Even today, the cocoa mass used is still prepared using different ingredients, including *cacao lavado*.

This term simply indicates that beans are taken straight from the pod, carefully washed, to get rid of the mucilage, then dried, without going through any other process!

In other words, unlike the cocoa from which chocolate as we know it has been made over the last few centuries, the cocoa which was the drink of the gods was not fermented.

Previous pages: in a cooperative in the region of Tabasco, the fermentation vats each contain approximately one ❯❯ thousand kilos of beans. Opposite, drying in the open air reduces the water content of the seed to between 5% and 7%. Following pages: left, fermented cocoa; right, *cacao lavado*, used in Mexico for drinks.

Bowl
or froth?

"(Las mazorcas) tienen de dentro los granos de cacao ; de fuera es morado y de dentro encarnado o bermejo. Cuando (el cacao) es nuevo, si se bebe mucho emborracha, y si se bebe templadamente refrigera y refresca."

Fray Bernardino de Sahagún, ± 1550

In most traditional drinks, cocoa is mixed with corn. Above, froth (*espuma*) is a refinement in the method of serving.

What did the first cocoa lovers do when they opened the pods they had taken down from the tree trunks? After opening the fruit, they must have tasted its flesh and realized that, not only was it not toxic, but it also gave off a pleasantly fresh aroma.

A second stage was reached when they added cold water to thin this white pulp and the seeds wrapped in it. After filtering it, they drank it as a kind of fruit juice sometimes called cocoa water.

In addition, the pulp being sweet, it is highly likely that the first alcoholic fermentation it underwent was spontaneous rather than intentional – as must have been its effect on those who consumed it.

All the rest, that is, the use of cocoa beans and their transformation into a mixture which would become the precursor of chocolate, is lost in the mists of time. But all the evidence suggests that the point of departure was the elaboration of a more or less liquid drink.

It is impossible to broach this subject in Central America without mentioning a foodstuff which is the basis of everyday cooking: corn.

Imagine a recipe in which the ingredients are water – as much as is required – one kilo of corn and two tablespoons of quicklime. This preparation – *nixtamal* – is part of the modern culinary heritage of several regions of Mexico and is featured in all good cookbooks.

In their *True History of Chocolate*, Sophie and Michael D. Coe get in on the act and trace the origins of this preparation, which goes back to the time of the Olmecs, some 2,000 years ago.

By that time, a certain number of edible plants had already been domesticated, including kidney beans, marrows, peppers, avocadoes and corn. In the case of the last of these, the first indications of its use go back nearly 5,000 years!

It was, however, during the second millennium BC that the process of nixtamalization was perfected. Until this discovery, Olmec cooks simply boiled their grains of

Cooking corn with quicklime to make it more digestible is a practice that goes back about 4,000 years, to the time **»** of the Olmecs.

corn and then ground them on millstones.

What did they add? Lime, ashes and roasted snail shells have all been suggested.

Whatever its origin, the addition of an alkaline substance, as well as the leaving of the corn in the cold overnight, made it possible to separate the grain from its pericarp, that is, its transparent outer shell. Corn became easier to grind and reduce to an appetizing mixture, and – as was demonstrated much later – the final product gained in nutritional value.

Why approach the subject of cocoa-based drinks by discussing the cooking of corn? Quite simply because corn is involved in many stimulating drinks – or liquid dishes – the kind that the peasants take with them for a day of toil in the fields.

Let us dwell for a moment on one of the most famous of these beverages, which is also one of the emblems of the culinary tradition of Tabasco: *pozol*. As described in a recent book entitled *Chocolate regalo del edén*, its preparation requires one kilo of corn, three litres of water, one tablespoon of quicklime and 250 grams of roasted and peeled cocoa.

This recipe was described more than four centuries ago, in about 1560, by Diego de Landa Calderón, the then bishop of Yucatán. In his *Relación de las Cosas de Yucatán*, he wrote: "Using corn and ground cocoa, they make a very tasty kind of froth, with which they celebrate their festivals."

It is worth noting in passing that, to characterize the froth, Landa uses the Spanish word *espuma*, the same word the Catalan chef Ferran Adriá gives to his concoctions squeezed through a siphon.

To the basic ingredients of corn and cocoa, spices may be added. In a work of reference, the appendices to the dictionary of the Spanish Royal Academy, the author describes *posol* (spelt with an *s*) as: "A nutritious and refreshing drink, elaborated from corn which has been boiled, roughly ground, dissolved and whisked in cold water, then mixed with sugar, as well as cocoa, annatto and roasted *zapote* seeds, the whole thing previously ground..."

This practice of adding spices to the drink is described in several documents dating from the early days of colonization. In 1571, Alonso de Molina published his Spanish and Mexican vocabulary, a bilingual dictionary of the Nahuatl language, which is still a standard reference work today. As evidence of the lexicographical precision of that language, every preparation which includes cocoa is given a specific name.

- *Pizòya* means "a fruit resembling (coastal) pine cones, which is consumed as a drink."
- *Niçapizòya*: "a drink made of these with water."
- *Niçapizòya quiña*: "cocoa in this manner with peppers."
- *Niçapizòyachina*: "cocoa in this manner with perfumed things."
- *Tocançapizòyachina*: "cocoa in this manner to be drunk when it is covered" – which seems to refer to froth, the famous *espuma* of the period.

Twenty years earlier, in about 1550, the Franciscan Bernardino de Sahagún, author of the Florence Codex, had described *xochiaya cacautl* as "a drink of chocolate with honey, prepared with dried flowers ground into powder." It is worth

From *achiote*, or annatto, a reddish colouring agent is extracted and used in cosmetics. As a condiment, it has an earthy taste.

noting in passing that the New World did not need to wait for Spanish influence to add sweetening to cocoa-based drinks.

According to botanists, this powder made from dried flowers has three different ingredients. In Spanish, one of them bears the name *orejuelas*, because of the shape of the thick, plump petals of the flower of the *Cymbopetalum penduliflorum*. This tree from the annona family (like the custard-apple) is known in Nahuatl by the name *xochinacaztle*. It grows in Mexico, especially in Veracruz and Chiapas. When dried, its flower tastes like black pepper with a hint of resin.

The other two components of this seasoning are *mecaxóchitl*, whose flower tastes like black pepper with a touch of aniseed, and *tlixochitl*, which is none other than vanilla.

Other indigenous species can be used in the preparation of cocoa-based drinks. Peppers (*Pimienta gorda*, for example) are often mentioned by the Mayas. *Achiote*, or annatto, is more intriguing. From the red

seeds contained in the spiny shell of the shrub *Bixa orellana*, a natural colouring agent (E 160b) is extracted and used in the cosmetics industry for lipstick, hence its vernacular name in English: lipstick tree. These seeds, which have a high fat content, can also be used as a condiment, giving food an earthy, musky taste.

In the region of Tabasco, the pit from another fruit, the coloured *zapote* (*Pouteria sapota*), is also used as a spice in chocolate-flavoured drinks, such as tejate. The *Pouteria sapota* tree can reach a height of twenty to forty metres and is native to the south of Mexico, where it may also provide the shade required by the cocoa tree. Its fruit is easily recognizable from its shape – that of a small rugby ball – and its orange skin. Sometimes incorrectly called *mamey* – which is the name of one of its cousins – the *zapote* is delicious raw : its creamy flesh is a curious mixture of pumpkin, sweet potato and maraschino cherry. Its pit, called a *pixte*, has to be roasted before

being ground into powder.

After this little shopping list of ingredients, it is time to consider cooking equipment. Even though modernization, in the form of electricity, has reached the remotest parts of the countryside, a fair number of cooks still use age-old utensils such as the *comal* and the *metate*.

When it comes to techniques, especially culinary ones, nothing can take the place of a demonstration by an expert on the subject. You have to see the process close up to grasp the manual dexterity which makes all the difference!

That day there were two experts, both inhabitants of the village of Muxupip. For the occasion, Catalina Chin Pech and Dolorosa May Martin were wearing the *terno*, the traditional Maya festive costume: a white dress with floral motifs sewn on the front.

Throughout Central America, from Nicaragua to Mexico, the making of chocolate follows immutable principles. The cocoa is first roasted on a *comal*.

Derived from the Nahautl word *comâlli*, the *comal* evokes the slab – originally of terra cotta – on which corn tortillas were baked, and which was also used for roasting grains of corn, cocoa beans, green coffee, peppers, and so on.

For generations of cooks, the *comal* has been a thick, flat cast-iron griddle, approximately fifty centimetres in diameter. Families hold on to them for a long time, and a good *comal* is handed down from mother to daughter. The older it is, the better it is at transmitting heat.

On this *comal*, the cocoa beans were not alone. In Muxupip, they are roasted with cinnamon bark, rather than with the indigenous aromatic vegetables described 450 years ago. At the end of this operation, which took about an hour, Catalina and Dolorosa removed the husks from the beans. It is worth mentioning in passing that the same principle of roasting is an essential stage in the manufacture of chocolate coating, before the peeled and broken beans are put in the conche.

The ground pit of the *zapote* was one of the indigenous condiments used in the making of chocolate. Nowadays, **»** it has been replaced by cinnamon, brought at a very early stage from Asia by the colonists. Cocoa and cinnamon have to be roasted to bring out the "chocolate" aroma.

It still remained to grind the beans and the cinnamon in order to make a mixture, the basis of the future chocolate-flavoured drink. It was here that one of the monuments of the paraphernalia of Mexican cooking played its part: the *metate*.

It can easily be observed that the *metate* often occupies a central place in kitchens and that, more than just an everyday object, it is part of the popular culture of Central America. Inseparable from its *mano* (the stone cylinder which the cook grips), the *metate* is officially (!) defined as an instrument used by women to grind the corn or *nixtamal* for tortillas and *pozol*. It is also used to reduce to powder all other ingredients requiring a similar operation: spices, cocoa, roasted coffee, and so on.

There are several types of *metate*. Some have feet or tripods, some do not. I must admit to preferring the simpler ones – those without feet – just as I prefer the older ones, those that have accompanied generations of cooks: women who have polished and repolished the stone with their repetitive gestures.

Meanwhile, our two experts had been busy for hours, getting one kilo of cocoa ready for the magic moment: the formation of the chocolate-flavoured mixture.

This transformation was gradual. First, the beans were ground to a powder, becoming ever finer with every movement of the women's arms. This movement generated heat, which was transmitted to the cocoa butter contained in the mass, so that it started to melt and create the chocolate. For the reaction to take place, a catalyst was required: a few drops of water added at regular intervals.

The pastilles that resulted were placed

The *metate*, the traditional grinder of Central America. Previous pages: Catalina and Dolorosa in festive Mayan costume, making chocolate.

Above, made from a shrub, the *jicara* bowl is still in everyday use as a container. Previous pages: Catalina and Dolorosa in festive Mayan costume, making chocolate. The *molinillo* on the chocolate pot is used for mixing the paste with water to produce froth.

on brown wrapping paper, where they waited to be transformed into a drink, with or without corn, *achiote* and other traditional ingredients. For this final stage, they used a *batidora* to mix the chocolate and the water, and a traditional bowl, a *jicara*, to serve the richly deserved beverage. But let us leave our two demonstrators for a moment and go back in time, at least as far back as the techniques of historical research allow.

It will be agreed that no liquid deserves to be called a drink without the containers in which to serve it. In this case, the few which have been saved have helped us to understand why this drink was considered the drink of the gods, and why it was served in such luxurious gold containers – something that fascinated the first eyewitnesses during the period of colonization.

Research into these civilizations – which goes far beyond the delicious but restricted context of cocoa – is made more difficult by the scarcity of written texts. As we have seen, the vast majority of them – the codices of the pre-Colombian period – were burned between 1560 and 1562, on the orders of the Grand Inquisitor of the New World, Bishop Diego de Landa.

Among those testimonies that have survived, it is worth taking a closer look, for example, at a number of codices compiled on the initiative of priests, in other words, after the arrival of Cortés. Dating from 1553, the Tudela Codex shows a frequently reproduced image. It is of a Nahua woman in fine clothes, which suggests she is of high social rank. She is decanting a liquid from a bowl – probably a *jicara* – which she is holding level with her face into another which is on the ground. This liquid is a cocoa-based drink, which she is trying to make frothy. Sophie and Michael Coe mention a similar figure on a painted vase of Mayan origin, dating from 800 years before this codex.

This kind of information, taken together with the many writings which mention *espuma*, certainly provides food for thought. It now seems certain that the consumption of cocoa-based drinks was more like a "chocolate ceremony" than our breakfast croissant accompanied by a cup of hot milky chocolate. There are several indications that this "froth theory" should be taken seriously, from the carvings on terra cotta bowls to the shape of the bowls themselves. There existed, for example, containers fitted with spouts, which made it possible to blow air into the liquid to produce froth. The servant would then pour the drink into bowls and, with the help of a tortoiseshell spoon, would deposit the froth on the surface of the liquid.

Centuries later, at the beginning of the third millennium, the very idea of froth still fascinates contemporary chefs. With or without the help of lecithin from soy beans as an emulsifying agent, it is considered good taste to place on the plate a cloud of little bubbles of foam, sometimes just called "air", in the manner of Ferran Adriá.

Over the last few decades, several researchers have put forward the theory that the popular pharmacopoeia may have included certain natural emulsifying agents. In Oaxaca, a climbing plant answering to the name of *Popozocamecatl* was used. Various Mayan texts refer to a plant known to the Lacandons, which made it possible to produce a stable froth, by whipping a drink made from corn and cocoa with the help of a whisk. This plant, rich in saponins, is also a climber, and its name can be spelt either *suguir* or *ajsukir*.

Would this expedition let me throw light on the matter? To set my mind at rest, all I had to do was plunge into the Lacandon jungle, which enjoys the status of a biosphere reserve. What made this prospect all the more delightful to me was the fact that the Lacandon jungle contains specimens of *criollo* cocoa trees, which are either wild in origin or even completely wild.

In the Lacandon jungle, Nakin Kin looking for *suguir*, a climbing plant known to have emulsifying properties. »

Made with corn, cocoa and *suguir*, the chocolate-flavoured drink of the Lacandons produces a very stable froth. The makeshift *batidora* is part of an ear of corn.

And fortune smiled on me. I had spotted on a map a *campamiento* called Río Lacanja, situated on the banks of the river of the same name. Built like a miniature *pueblo*, the *campamiento* welcomes passing tourists who are interested in ecological walking tours and offers them basic lodgings in the form of cabins on the banks of the river. Close to the open-air restaurant is a craft shop selling objects and jewellery made from plant material. It was there that I met Nakin Kin, a lady whose name means "House of the Sun".

Her name proved justified when I said the only word we might possibly have in common: *suguir*. The password worked. Barefoot, Nakin Kin led me along a path in the jungle and, after a few hundred metres, looked up at the sky, repeating in her guttural dialect the word *suguir*, *suguir*. There indeed was our *suguir*, reaching seven to eight metres in height.

Impervious to the thorns on this climber, Nakin Kin used all her strength to bring the heads of the leaves and the fruits – little red berries – within reach.

I had had the bright idea of bringing some already roasted cocoa beans with me. Nakin Kin ground them – in an electric mill, the kind used to grind corn. She then mixed this magic potion with a little water. Then, using a *molinillo* she had made herself, she whisked the liquid. In a few minutes, the froth appeared, perfectly stable, and she spooned it into a large plastic bowl. The whole of Mexico, its history and its colours, was concentrated in those few bubbles, which, according to my temporary culinary guide, remain stable for days on end.

The last word should go to the *molinillo*. It consisted of a stick onto which Nakin Kin had attached part of an ear of corn! From the *molinillo* to the *chocolatière* is not a big step, and we can take that step in the village of Dzitya, not far from Mérida, a village renowned in the whole of Mexico for its woodwork.

Juan Elías Canché is a specialist in making the *batidora*: the traditional Yucatán version of the *chocolatière* or chocolate pot beloved of Madame de Pompadour, who, we may recall, was the first person in France to commission a chocolate service in porcelain. Her *chocolatière* was also fitted with a small wooden mill which answered to the name *moussoir*, or froth maker. Yet another reference to *espuma*!

Juan Elías does not use porcelain but hard, thick wood. Made from the wood of the guayacán tree, the *batidora* certainly requires dexterity. But it is the *molinillo*, made from a branch of besinnache wood, which is even more spectacular. As the final stage of his work, Juan makes a ring from the end of this branch, a disc which is free to move while still being attached. This accessory, as we may suspect, is intended to help in making froth.

The existence of this craft leaves open a question on the origins of the *batidora* and its *molinillo*. Were these accessories born in the New World, given that the creation of froth represented a kind of culinary consecration?

Apparently not. In fact, the first models of chocolate pots – with a lid and a spout – appear in Spanish paintings from 1630, a full century after the fall of Tenochtitlán. The presence of both the pot and the froth maker in these still lifes indicates that the Hispanic nobility and middle classes had already adopted chocolate-flavoured drinks.

It was from Europe, then, that the chocolate pot and the froth maker were imported into Central America. Before that, as a reading of Alonso de Molina's Spanish-Nahuatl dictionary shows, no word existed to describe either the *batidora* or its *molinillo*.

Times had certainly changed since the Milanese adventurer Guillermo Benzoni wrote of cocoa in the middle of the 16th century: "It is more like a drink for pigs than for humans. I was in the country (Nicaragua) for more than a year and never wanted to taste it."

In the intervening years, the conquered had persuaded the conquerors that cocoa had beneficial effects on their virility. Clearly, this unusual marketing ploy worked a treat.

« Just as in the past, chocolate is served with a surface covering of froth, the local *espuma*. Following pages: the chocolate pot, although made in the land of the Mayas, was invented in Europe early in the 17th century.

The sacred gardens of Yucatán

"Al presente son tant ingeniosos los Indios deste Obispo... Todos en general tienen sus tierras amojonadas y heredades. Y los Cupules (de Valladolid) tienen huertas que llaman Zenotes o Hoias donde cultivan el cacao."

don Pedro Sánchez de Aguilar, ± 1610

Opposite, the famous sacred *cenote* of Chichén Itzá. Above, the lush vegetation of the *cenote* of Popolá.

The Mayan civilization means cocoa. That much has been established. And cocoa means a natural zone of expansion. This is a part of the world where the cocoa tree finds the ideal climatic conditions for its growth: the right temperature, the right humidity, and so on. The furthest limits of this zone are situated roughly at the level of the 20th parallel, on either side of the equator.

There are some important Mayan cities, located in the northern part of Yucatán, which hover around this 20th parallel. Chichén Itzá, for example, is at 20°40' north.

Does that mean that cocoa was cultivated in Yucatán? That is a question which many anthropologists and botanists have asked themselves. They have found the answer in the form of slender cocoa trees planted in large natural pits. The history of these pits begins a very long time ago, with an asteroid: 298 Baptistina.

Why am I talking about an asteroid in a book about cocoa – Mexican cocoa, to boot? The connection is a distant one, but the explanation is quite simple. About 160 million years ago, this asteroid, 160 kilometres in diameter, collided with another heavenly body, 60 kilometres in diameter. The two bodies exploded, creating tens of thousands of meteorites. One of the biggest of these measured 10 kilometres in diameter. About 65 million years ago, it came down off the Yucatán Peninsula and produced a crater, 200 kilometres in diameter, known as the Chicxulub Crater, from the name of a town near Mérida, the capital of Yucatán.

This meteorite played a decisive role in the evolution of the animal world. It has

The region of Chichén Itzá has a damper climate than the rest of Yucatán and includes many *cenotes*, often called sacred orchards or gardens.

been held responsible for the disappearance of a large number of species, from the ammonites to the dinosaurs...

It is almost impossible to imagine the heat there must have been on earth at that moment. The energy given off by the impact was immeasurable, five billion times that of the Hiroshima bomb. This thermic phenomenon caused the vaporization of enormous quantities of water, as well as the melting of adjacent rocks.

From a climatological point of view, it can be classed as a mega tsunami, the waves of which reached several thousand metres in height. Under the impact of such a blast and such exceptional heat, the sub-soil of Yucatán was literally transformed into a giant Emmenthal cheese (Gruyère does not have holes!). A karstic landscape was formed, with an underground network of caves, of which the longest, discovered only recently, spreads over 160 kilometres.

This 160 million-year-old landscape evolved – on the geological scale of time – bringing about, for example, the formation of dolines, or sinkholes. These geological accidents are caused by the decay – or collapse – of crumbly limestone terrain, rocky crusts on the surface of what were previously the vaults of underground cavities.

A doline can be understood as a cave which has been left exposed to the open air. It usually continues to be supplied with fresh water by an underground stream. Dozens of these great open-air pits can be found in the Yucatán Peninsula. The Mayas gave them the name dz'onot – later Hispanized as cenote.

Of all the cenotes, the best known is in the ancient city of Chichén Itzá. As John Lloyd Stephens noted in his *Incidents of Travel in Yucatán*, this site is considered a sacred cenote and a place where human sacrifices were performed.

More prosaically, these cenotes have naturally given access to reserves of fresh water. It is highly likely that the Mayan cities of Yucatán were only able to develop by taking advantage of these.

To agronomists, the cenotes also represent the only microcosm in which cocoa was able to grow in the arid soil of Yucatán, a soil more suitable for growing henequén – sisal – elaborated from Agave fourcroydes, than a tree whose original habitat was the tropical rainforest.

But the region of Chichén Itzá, which is in the north of Yucatán, is the one exception, having a higher rainfall than elsewhere (between 1,000 and 1,500 millimetres per year). In addition, the region is riddled with dozens of these great pits, these cenotes, in which water still rises to the surface, although only to a limited extent – in fact, it may be totally absent.

On the other hand, there is ground water fairly close to the surface, and the roots of the trees often only have to go down a few metres to reach it.

All the written texts, such as those of Sánchez de Aguilar, an eye-witness of the colonial period, describe these cultivated lands as gardens, insisting on the lushness of their vegetation.

Being the enthusiast for the history of cocoa that he is, Mathieu Brees has explored several dozen cenotes, beginning with those in which cocoa trees were previously discovered. Many of these trees have disappeared, thanks to two tropical cyclones, Gilberto in 1988 and Isodoro in 2002. The second of these caused flooding

In the cenote of Popolá, some fifteen young cocoa trees have been counted. Following pages: Underground water **»** has reappeared in Popolá, forming a pond.

on an unprecedented scale: the water took months to recede, and in the *cenotes* that were affected, the cocoa trees simply vanished.

As an educational introduction to the subject, Mathieu proposed to show me two *cenotes* in the region of Valladolid. For my part, I entertained the hope of finding a *criollo* cocoa pod, or even a wild cocoa tree descended from the first trees brought to Mesoamerica.

In order to visit the first of these *cenotes*, we arranged to meet Alex, a young man from the village of Popolá, situated halfway between Chichén Itzá and Yaxuná. He guided us to the site of this remarkable garden, a microcosm with many points of interest. With the help of an abseiling rope, we easily descended into its bowels.

Unlike the sacred *cenote* of Chichén, the *cenote* of Popolá is only partly in the open air, because part of the vault of the ancient cave did not collapse. On this side of the *cenote*, one section, perhaps a quarter of the ground surface, is made up of stagnant water. The rest is covered in a soil incredibly rich in humus, in which a varied assortment of trees and shrubs grows, including large specimens of *pimienta gorda* (often sold under the name Jamaica pepper), which bear fruits with a round seed. On them are climbing plants, including several feet of indigenous vanilla.

Interesting as these two spices were, they were not sufficient reason to justify going down into this *cenote*. We were looking for cocoa trees and we found them: large and small, young and old, some fifteen in all.

Unfortunately, there was not the small-

est pod to be seen, let alone a flower. Mathieu and I had to leave frustrated. We had no idea if these trees were *criollos*, let alone if they were the descendents of a wild plant acclimatized here many moons ago...

The second *cenote* of the day took us into another world. Situated in the village of Xocén, it is known by the name of Aktun Sitio. Mathieu had previously tried several times to locate it, but unsuccessfully, having been refused access by the elders of Xocén, who were anxious to protect this sacred site.

To understand this not very hospitable attitude, it is important to realize that Xocén has a remarkable claim to fame, in that it houses the Santissima Cruz Tun. The presence of this miraculous cross marks the village as the centre of the world, and a mixture of Catholic worship and Mayan legend has grown up around it.

The mystery surrounding Xocén and its *cenote* intrigued a researcher named Arturo Gómez-Pompa and two of his colleagues. Having examined three *cenotes* in the region, they published their findings in 1990 in the revue *Latin American Antiquity*, under the title "The sacred cocoa woods of the Mayas".

We managed to reach our goal by poaching two young boys whom we found perched on the same bicycle. Leaving their vehicle on the track, they took us to the edge of the precipice.

Aktun Sitio, like the sacred *cenote* of Chichén Itzá, is a large circular hole. It is 40 metres deep and 150 metres in diameter. Its very steep sides make it difficult to explore. When we expressed the desire to go down into it, our makeshift guides assured us that there was no way in...

Arturo Gómez-Pompa had obviously had better luck, since he was able to publish an outline of the ligneous vegetation of this *cenote*, identifying fifteen kinds of tree and shrubs.

More than fifteen years later, we were

A cocoa and a *zapote*, two of the large trees in the *cenote* of Aktun Sitio.

able to confirm his observations, finding ourselves confronted with the tops of plants identical in every way to those he described. Among them, in the shade of a *zapote* (*Pouteria mammosa*), there grew a cocoa tree. And there, high on this cocoa tree, was a fruit, a single pod, visible to the naked eye. Seeing the slender nature of the tree, our young guides estimated its height at one *mecate*, an Aztec measurement equivalent to 21.78 metres, that is, six centimetres less than the earlier Mayan measure, the *kaan*.

The colour of the pod – light green mixed with purple – its slightly elongated shape and its somewhat pronounced ribs certainly suggested it was a *criollo*.

Unable to reach this fruit and check the colour of its seeds, we were forced to be content with guesswork. Out of respect for our guides and their beliefs, we decided not to go down into Aktun Sitio.

But we came away with the certainty that others before us had gained access,

beginning with those who had grown their orchard in it. For if we look at the list published in *Latin American Antiquity*, we can see that among the plants growing in this little piece of managed forest are not only indigenous species such as *Mangifera indica* (the mango tree) or *Brosimum alicastrum* (the breadnut tree), but also plants foreign to the region: the banana tree, the orange tree and the coconut palm.

The man
who loves trees

« Le but (du livre : L'homme qui plantait des arbres) était de faire aimer l'arbre ou plus exactement de faire aimer à planter des arbres (ce qui est depuis toujours une de mes idées les plus chères). »

Jean Giono, 1957

Tito Adán Jiménez Rodríguez and his daughter Mónica on their *rancho* La Concepción, near Pichucalco. Both have a passion for trees and practise a kind of forest agriculture which has been certified as biological.

Our car had been following Tito's car for several kilometres now. We had left the very unremarkable centre of Pichucalco and followed an asphalted main road. Halfway up a hill, our guide stopped his covered Nissan pick-up truck at the side of the track and invited us to join him. Much to my surprise, he asked us to place in a row the white plastic garden chairs which he had made ready for the day's guests. And so it was that the little group which Mathieu and I had joined got into the back of the vehicle. It was like being in an improvised minibus.

Tito Adán Jiménez Rodríguez seems older than the 74 years his birth certificate claims. In Chiapas and well beyond Central America, he is regarded with a great deal of respect, and taken as a point of reference. Gradually he is passing the torch to his daughter Mónica.

Geographically, Pichucalco is the epicentre of an enclave of the state of Chiapas within the territory of the state of Tabasco. Unlike in other states of Mexico, the word *hacienda* is rarely used here. A farm, whether it raises crops or livestock, is called a *rancho*.

Some explain this by the fact that colonial influence was less strong here, the Indians of the region having put up a stiff resistance to the intruders who had come to conquer their country in the 16 th century.

As we were tossed about on those makeshift seats in the back of the truck, the landscape unfurled before our eyes. Whenever the road was not hemmed in by steep sides, we caught glimpses of magnificent green hills. The grass in the meadows was so thick as to look very lush.

Typical landscape in the region of Pichucalco, Chiapas. »

On the way to Tito's ranch, La Concepción, Tito did not talk to me about cocoa,
but about trees in general. More than a
farmer, Tito is a forester at heart. He
stopped the vehicle for a moment to
explain to me the techniques for extracting latex from the indigenous rubber tree,
the *hule*. Tito is one of the few landown-
ers still doggedly exploiting this species,
which answers to the highly appropriate
Latin name of *Castilloa elastica*.

As in much of the state of Chiapas, the
agricultural resources of Pichucalco are
centred on coffee, which has overtaken
cocoa in importance. More recently, the
banana has made a dramatic appearance
on the scene. Things are developing very
quickly: covetous eyes have been cast on
the petroleum in the sub-soil. Until now,
pumping it has been too expensive, but
the steep rise in the cost of crude oil has
altered the game.

The pick-up finally stopped. Tito
pointed up at some trees overrun with a
creeper whose foliage was as beautiful as
it was abundant. Scattered over his plantations, the indigenous vanilla originally
from Veracruz – for that is what it is –
brings him in a decent income every year.

Like this vanilla, all Tito's agricultural
activities are at the opposite extreme
from Porfirio's well ordered orchards at
La Joya. La Concepción and the other
properties belonging to this family are
laid out like a managed forest. One might
almost feel as if one were transported
back 1,500 years, to the times when the
Mayas first started domesticating cocoa
trees. I was later to learn that, apart from
the forest species, some ornamental flowers and some species of precious wood
are also exploited.

It was not very late in the afternoon,
and yet the light was already fading. We
had just enough time left to walk across
the plantation and gaze at the sunset from
the other side of the hill. The path we took
rose and fell – differences in level which
could not have made the crops easy to
maintain or harvest. Clearly, no tractor or
mechanized vehicle could enter without
causing serious damage and shattering the
fragile balance of these tropical biotopes.

To find out more and get answers to all
our questions, we agreed to meet the following morning. That meant we still had
three journeys to make – one and a half
return trips – sitting on plastic chairs,
bumping about on the rough track.

We returned the next day to find that
Mónica, Tito's right arm, had organized
everything perfectly. Young Tomas, one
of their workers, was waiting for us, holding part of a branch from an orange tree,
which he sharpened to make a kind of
skewer. It would help him to pollinate the
flowers of the vanilla plant. These flowers
are shaped like deep trumpets and insects
cannot get all the way inside to complete
the pollination process. For a long time,
bees were charged with this task, but
pesticides eventually put paid to them...
Tomas made an incision in the calyx,
removed the pollen and closed the flower
again, before moving on to the next one.

Meanwhile, Moctezuma, the foreman
of La Concepción, guided us through the
25 varieties of cocoa which grow in a joy-
ful – and probably only apparent – confu-
sion on the plantation. His young son was
with him, clearly proud to be carrying
his big machete.

Since the end of the 1990s, Tito has been
renewing the population of cocoa trees on

Tomas, with two types of *uranga* cocoa pods. Above, a cocoa of the *trinitario* type.

his plantation, grafting on clones and selected varieties.

At this point, I must admit to being confused by the agronomic vocabulary of the different regions of Mexico. In my mind, and according to the dictionary, a clone is the total of the individuals obtained without pollination from a single individual. But when Tito and Mónica talked to me about their clonal *uranga*, all I could see were pods so different in shape and colour that they could not possibly have come from the same parent. Admittedly, they do all have one family resemblance: a very verrucose skin, quite pleasant to the touch. It was a mystery I was not to solve. But do these academic debates really matter, when the product is so good, even excellent?

This *uranga* cocoa is one of the commercial spearheads of Arroyo el Afiladero, the company run by Tito and his daughters. The seeds contained in the pods are irregular, thinner at the two ends and fatter in the middle. Such disparities in the size of the beans make fermentation a more complex process, since the heat produced during the process penetrates a small bean more quickly than a large one.

The cotyledons are usually white, but about 20% of the beans are pink on the inside. On this basis, the *uranga* is not considered in the region to be a *criollo*, even though, according to the canons of botanical taxonomy, it answers all the criteria. That is another mystery I have no desire to elucidate.

The *uranga* is not Don Tito's only pride. He showed me two other cocoa cultivars: the ceylan – a *forastero* variety – and the *blanco marfil*. The seeds of the latter are spotlessly white. It is generally agreed to be a true *criollo*, and, what is more, it is about 60% cocoa butter, as against a maximum of 50% for the *uranga*.

When their respective seeds are roasted, the flavours are very different. With the *uranga*, the darker beans release a highly scented flavour of flowers of the fields. The *blanco marfil* is softer, more delicate.

To compare it with a wine, it has the subtlety of a *pinot noir*. The *ceylan*, on the other hand, is full-flavoured, with a touch of acidity reminiscent of coffee.

In order to produce such distinct aromatic compounds, fermentation is a vital stage in the process, and here, too, Tito is accepted as an authority.

He does his fermentation in 800-kilo casks, made from American cedarwood. The total duration of this physico-chemical transformation varies from 96 hours for a *blanco marfil* to 128 hours in the case of an *uranga*. But bringing this stage to a satisfactory end requires a certain tact, to determine exactly when to turn over the mass and when to stop fermentation and move on to drying.

Mónica knows the value of what her father has achieved and the quality of the cocoas elaborated. But she insisted, "Our cocoa isn't the best. There are many good cocoas in this country, each with its own aroma, its own flavour. Quite simply, our soil gives it a unique flavour."

Another detail worth mentioning is that the cocoas on this farm are certified as being produced using biological agriculture. We are close here to the principles of biodynamics, since all the operations of sewing and harvesting follow the phases of the moon.

We left the plantation to find a surprise waiting for us. The soft light of morning had given way to an already burning sun. Mónica had thrown together a breakfast which was more like a brunch. Tomas, Moctezuma and his son joined us in a meal of tortillas, *frijoles*, grilled sausages and plantain chips.

They drew their machetes and, with a few precise blows, took the tops off some coconuts, which had been kept cool in the morning dew.

Señor Tito Adán Jiménez Rodríguez, I can just imagine you in the role of the character Elzéard Bouffier, the man who spent all his life planting trees, as created by Jean Giono.

Previous pages: pods: from left to right, *criollo*, *guayaquil* (*forastero*), green *trinitario*, two *uranga* and *criollo* »
blanco marfil. Opposite, a red *uranga* pod and its mixture of beans: red and purplish crimson.

Criollo
and neocriollo

*"I really think that in this country (Trinidad)
we have nothing which we can offer you better
than you already have in Central America."*

Mr. Williams, 1943

Clara María Echeverría, her husband Porfirio, and their granddaughter Christell, on the *hacienda* La Joya, known for the *neocriollo* cocoa selected by Clara's father.

Clara María Echeverría Hernandez is proud to show off a letter dated February 13 1942, a letter which is part of her family history and the history of cocoa in Tabasco. It is a reply by the director of agriculture in Trinidad to a question her father, Carlos Echeverría Valenzuela, had addressed to the body researching cocoa in Trinidad, which was known to have collected a large amount of genetic material. In this material, Carlos was hoping to discover the miracle clone that might resist the greatest disease of the cocoa tree, witches' broom, caused by the tiny fungus *Crinipellis perniciosa*.

If he could get rid of this plague, Carlos Echeverría hoped to be able to increase the yield of his plantations and contribute to the resurgence of cocoa in Tabasco.

At the beginning of the 1940s, this region, once so famous for its cocoa, was struggling to emerge from a crisis of unprecedented severity that had already lasted more than twenty years. The general political situation was bad, a chaotic agrarian reform was under way, and there was uncertainty as to the future of privately owned land. On the international market, cocoa produced in Mexico faced strong competition from African cocoas. The harvest of 1933 had been the worst in modern times: a mere 500 tonnes, as compared with, for example, 2,655 in 1941, 30,000 in 1963 and 55,880 in 1993!

Following the advice of his correspondent in the Caribbean, Don Carlos decided to look for the gem he needed closer to home, in Chontalpa, the great historical cocoa-producing area. Here he identified a tree bearing finer, healthier pods than

Born in a highly agricultural region, Porfirio has increased the density of his cocoa tree plantation to 800 plants per ›› hectare. Gathering is done with a *luco*, a long pole fitted with a sharp blade.

those of its neighbouring cocoa trees. He decided to make it his benchmark "variety" and called it C1, an abbreviation of Carmelo 1, after his *hacienda*, El Carmelo, situated at Río Seco.

Carlos classified it as a *neocriollo*, because it had the white seed (in the trade it is called an almond) of a *criollo*, as well as the same flavour and the same aroma, while giving a greater yield. Its resistance to disease also proved to be greater.

Regarded by his peers as an unconventional planter, Echeverría decided to graft all the trees on his estate with this clone. It was a far costlier operation than growing new trees in a nursery from seedlings. But he was able to harvest the first of these new pods much earlier, after only two years. The results were impressive: according to official statistics, the average yield per hectare in the area was 430 kilos, but Carlos Echeverría declared that he had produced 4.7 kilos of beans per tree, which, multiplied by the 400 cocoa trees in one hectare, gave a total of 1,880 kilos!

Carlos had two children, one of whom was Clara María. Clara's brother having squandered the family inheritance, she and her husband Porfirio started again from scratch, at La Joya, their *hacienda* situated not far from Río Seco, at Cunduacan.

Porfirio's character is the opposite of his wife's. Where she is dynamic, a bundle of nervous energy, he is reserved. He walked slowly and silently towards me, his face shaded by his straw hat.

It was under the cocoa trees that Porfirio told me his story. He was not born in Chontalpa, but moved there from the state of Chihuahua in the north of Mexico.

His family were farmers, accustomed to large-scale agriculture. His first crop was sugar cane. But, aware of the potential of his father-in-law's C1 cocoa, Porfirio began with a small area of two hectares, hoping to enlarge it over time as the prices paid for the beans increased.

The straight rows, the well pruned trees and their open skeletal structures: all this reveals Porfirio's expertise. His skill as a farmer has allowed him to double the density of planting, increasing it to 800 trees per hectare.

Porfirio grabbed his machete and cut a pod in half. The blade sliced through the fresh seeds, revealing their flesh, those famous cotyledons which absolutely have to be between white and slightly pink for a pod to be a *criollo*. And so it proved!

He repeated the action with other pods. They all had white seeds. Except for one, which had a mixture of white and purple cotyledons. The flower which gave birth to it must have been pollinated by an insect which had removed the pollen from a *trinitario* or a *forastero*. That was the only exception.

Armed with their traditional *lucos*, the gatherers bring down pods in their thousands. Fermentation is done on the *hacienda*. Clara María exports some of her beans to the United States, Switzerland and Spain. In Belgium, they are used by Pierre Marcolini. As for myself, I have dedicated to this family one of my benchmark chocolates: pure Tabasco *criollo*.

Faced with a great product, we should be modest, which is what I tried to do in making this plain ganache and coating. Tasting reveals the floral character, the sweetness and the slightly caramel taste of the cocoa of La Joya.

The last time I met Porfirio, at home with his wife and his little girl Christell, he told me of his plan to enlarge the farm, doubling its area from five to ten hectares. Sadly, since then, I have learned that he has terminal cancer. There are days when we would like life to go on for everyone and never abandon exceptional people along the way.

Selected by Carlos Echeverría, the clone Carmelo 1 presents all the aspects of a *criollo*, including a large number **»** of seeds with white cotyledons.

Soconusco,
past glories rediscovered

"In the Soconusco, it is difficult to find criollos today, although many people say they have kept a few criollo trees for personal use because the flavor and overall quality of criollo cacao is perceived to be so much better than forastero."

Janine Gasco, *Chocolate in Mesoamerica*, 2006

At Tapachula, in the province of Soconusco, Samuel Guillén Díaz is one of the planters most active in the programme of participatory selection instituted by the University of Chiapas. He has selected three types of cocoa tree for his plantations.

In the Museum of Anthropology in Mexico City – probably the most remarkable museum of its kind in the world – the room devoted to Aztec society during the Mexica period (1325–1521) features a map showing the routes by which tribute was brought from the subject regions to the capital, Tenochtitlán.

This map traces the migration, across the whole country, of various major raw materials, such as cotton, precious metals, or cocoa, and is based on written texts of the period, according to which cocoa came mostly from Soconusco. It also emerges from these texts that this *criollo* cocoa was particularly prized, even more so than cocoa from Tabasco.

It is always amusing to research the etymology of words. For Soconusco, such an exercise must begin with the Mexican flag. Between the two stripes on either side – the green and the red – an eagle holds a writhing snake in its beak. To complete the scene, the king of raptors is perched on a prickly pear, in Latin *opuntia ficus-indica*. This is not a new image. In fact, it is found in several codices, including the Ramirez Codex, a document dating from the 16th century. Still known as Indian fig, the prickly pear, so prominently displayed in the eagle's claws, is in fact a cactus native to Mexico.

One only has to visit local markets to realise the importance of prickly pear. Nopal – to give it its local name – is widely used in popular cookery. The famous nopales are simply young prickly pears stripped of their sharp thorns and cooked like any other vegetable.

Why am I talking about nopal in an expedition entirely devoted to cocoa? Quite simply because in Nahuatl, the language spoken by the Aztecs, the fruit of the opuntia was called *xoconostle*. In all likelihood, it was the Spanish conquistadors who corrupted the word to Xoconochco and subsequently gave the name to a coastal region in the south of Mexico.

Provided one has a detailed map of the state of Chiapas, it is possible to locate a little *pueblo* that answers to the name of Soconusco, situated close to Route MEX 200, between Tapachula and Huixla.

On my visit to this community – it can hardly be called a village – I discovered, along an abandoned railway line, a building which, as its pediment indicated, once housed the cocoa producers' cooperative. Today, it is filled with crates of mangos belonging to those same producers, who have now switched to fruit farming. The farmers present that day told me that there is only one cocoa producer left in the area, most of the others having gone over to banana production.

From the evidence, it seemed impossible that the greatness of this region could once all have been concentrated in this one place. The fact is that the name Soconusco refers to much more than a *pueblo*. This province of the state of Chiapas, a province bordered by the Pacific, extends over more than 200 kilometres from north to south and 50 kilometres from east to west. Its borders even extend into Guatemala, as far as the outskirts of the capital city.

In order to grasp the historical importance of Soconusco, we must go back five hundred years. In his *Historia verdadera de la conquista de la Nueva España*, the great chronicler Bernal Díaz del Castillo writes that it took him eight to ten days to cross the region. That was in 1525, and his

In the Mendoza Codex, an eagle rests on a prickly pear, a plant from which the name Soconusco is derived. The same eagle, holding a snake in its beak, appears on the modern Mexican flag.

description of it suggests a paradise on earth. "The whole province is a garden filled with cocoa trees. The orchards, like the houses, are well maintained."

There are several reasons for such an idyllic picture, beginning with natural ones. According to specialists, there are few regions in the New World which display such a diversity of biotopes, going from sea level up to an altitude of more than 4,000 metres. Because of its latitude (between the 13th and 17th parallels), the coastal strip benefits from a tropical climate with a stable temperature, ranging from an average of 27°C in the coldest month to an average of 30°C in the hottest. As for the rainfall, it can be compared to that of a monsoon system. In short, it rains at least twice as much

as plants require.

These environmental conditions are similar to those of the native habitat of the cocoa tree. Historians and agronomists believe that Soconusco was one of the places through which the first plants were introduced into Mexico, and that it subsequently became the cradle of cocoa cultivation in Central America, probably from as early as 400 BC.

After the end of the pre-Colombian era, we no longer have to rely on guesswork. Various written texts of the time record the incredible economic vitality of the province of Soconusco.

Another illustrated book, the Mendoza Codex, written in 1541–1542, devotes 39 pages to a list of the goods paid as tribute by the conquered cities to the Aztecs. For the province of Soconusco, this inventory mentions precious stones such as amber, gold and jade, but also jaguar skins and finery made from bird feathers. Among the cultivated products, we find cocoa beans and containers for drinking, the ancestors of the *jicara*.

There is a theory among historians that the intrinsic value – not to mention the organoleptic qualities – of *criollo* cocoa from Soconusco was the principal reason for the subjugation of this province by the Aztecs. The taxes paid constituted a very large amount for the period: more than 4,000 kilos of dried beans per year.

Transporting goods in this way over hundreds of kilometres required an efficient transport system. Within the Aztec empire, this was the privilege of a particular caste, the *pochteca*, whose name means roughly "men of the land of the ceiba".

Here again we find the ceiba, that giant more than 40 metres high, which we encountered, among other places, in the Lacandon jungle. We may recall that this was the mythical tree of the Maya, a bridge for man between the underworld and the vault of heaven.

What did the *pochteca* do? They organised caravans of hundreds of porters leaving from the city of Tochtepec, a stopping-off point situated close to where Oaxaca now stands. It was there that the *pochteca* owned storehouses, from where they dispatched merchandise to the three great allied cities of the valley of Mexico: Tenochtitlán, Texcoco and Tlacopán.

In Tochtepec, this small army of porters, all travelling on foot, divided into two columns which set off southwards. The first made its way to the city of Xicallanco, on the Atlantic coast, near the present-day Ciudad del Carmen. The second column made for Xoconochco, on the Pacific coast. Transformed into security guards – cocoa was not only the drink of an elite but also a currency – they then set off on the return journey, each laden with 24,000 cocoa beans.

And if you want to practice your accounting skills, know that this figure – 24,000 seeds – is a reference to a unit of weight, the *xiquipilli*, which designates a sack containing 8,000 seeds. The load – the *carga* – of a porter therefore corresponded to 3 *xiquipilli*!

It did not take long for the Spanish conquistadors to discover the value of this region. Many writings from the colonial period, which lasted for three centuries – from 1519 to 1821 – describe the assets of the province of Soconusco, insisting on the great agricultural potential of this region due to the fertility of its soil.

It is known, among other things, that in 1548, the region paid the Spanish a tax equivalent to 200 *cargas* of cocoa beans, more or less exactly what it paid the Aztecs. In 1582, the town of Guilocingo alone included fifteen "Indians", heads of families, who each owned a plantation varying in size from 200 to 3,200 cacao trees.

This arrangement, that is, the payment in kind of part of the taxes in the form of cocoa beans, lasted for a whole two centuries.

An agricultural census carried out between 1819 and 1820, in other words, on the eve of independence, enumerated 424,819 productive trees in the province, for a population of 9,528. This was, however, less than a third of what had been cultivated at the beginning of the

It is in these orchards in the province of Soconusco that trees are selected whose yield and resistance to disease » are exceptional. They are then grafted onto cocoa trees with lower yields.

Samuel (with his brother Caralampio and his son Samuel) has selected a clone with red pods, which he has grafted onto many of the existing trees on his plantation.

16th century, when it is said there were about 1,500,000 cacao trees.

Having researched the epic story of cocoa from Xoconochco, I was anxious to go and meet today's *cacaoteros* – and their beans, which had been so prized over the centuries. But the existing literature on the subject, including a field study carried out at the beginning of this century by the anthropologist Janine Gasco, did not fill me with optimism. It seems that the official programmes to replace the original *criollos* by the more productive varieties of *forasteros* and *trinitarios* have wrought havoc, even there.

Based on the testimonies she gathered, Janine Gasco concludes that many trees believed to be *criollos* by their owners are not, in fact, *criollos* at all.

I was able to find out for myself when I met Samuel Guillén Diaz, a planter with an endearing personality. With his son, Samuel, and his brother, Caralampio, Samuel lives in Hidalgo, a hamlet near Tapachula, a city close to the border with Guatemala which proudly bears the name "The Pearl of Soconusco".

Mathieu Brees had organized a meeting on Samuel's plantation with two researchers from the independent university of Chiapas, Orlando López Báez and his wife Isabel Ramírez González.

The first thing I noticed, apart from the fabulous red pods on the cocoa trees, were the many ripe mangoes which had fallen from the tall mango trees that grow in the middle of his cocoa plantations.

Samuel, who sensed my fondness for food, let me taste them. They were warm, ripe, juicy, and incredibly delicious. The reputation of Soconusco and its exceptional climate was already proving to be well deserved!

A peasant at heart, Samuel takes good

care of his plantations. Few of his fruits, for example, are afflicted with moniliosis. But what struck me most was his determination, his force of character. He told me that, some years earlier, cocoa had brought in too little for a living wage. For a time, the 120 planters in the region had considered transforming their orchards into banana plantations. "But just as they were about to sign the contract," Samuel said, "we discovered that all the advantages were the other way."

It was here that Orlando López spoke up. An agricultural engineer, his guiding principle is that nothing can be done without the farmers. In his opinion, the green revolution begun in the developing world in the 1960s favoured farmers who had the means to buy improved plants, fertilizers, pesticides, and so on.

The others were left with their family properties, which often yielded less.

Orlando therefore devised a programme which he called "participatory selection".

It rested on a basic principle of genetics. In any given population, in this case a cocoa plantation, we find trees of which some are more worthwhile than others. It may be that they produce more, or that they have tastier fruit.

A first selection, made by going over the plantations with their owners, made it possible to pinpoint 400 worthwhile trees in two cocoa-producing areas of Tapachula. Reduced to 126 after a further evaluation, these were closely monitored for more than a year. Their pods, their resistance to disease, their content in seeds, the size of these seeds, and so on, were carefully recorded, making it possible to select 17 worthwhile trees, of which three grew on Samuel's plantation.

"It is important to note," Orlando said, "that the average tree currently yields half a kilo of dried beans per year. With the 17 trees which will be our future 'parents', the average varies from 2.13 to 4.77 kilos."

Samuel is particularly proud of one of

The fat content of the pods selected by Samuel is high, reaching 54%. As the purple colour of the seeds shows, »
they are probably a hybrid between a *criollo* cocoa and a *forastero* or a *trinitario*.

his varieties which has been selected. Some twenty pods of an old rose colour – the same colour as the polo shirt he was wearing that day – were hanging from a tree trunk.

With its slightly curved tip, this pod was reminiscent of the *cundeamor* type, in other words, a *criollo*. But when the pod was opened, the seeds turned out to be mauve in colour, whereas the identifying mark of a *criollo*, as we have seen, is that the cotyledons – which correspond to the flesh of the seeds – are whitish...

Both men considered it highly likely that these pods were produced by a spontaneous hybrid, the result of a cross between a *criollo* and a *forastero* or a *trinitario*.

"The seeds are big and round," Orlando said. "Analysis has shown that the fat content of the seeds is 54% of their weight, as against the average of 45 to 46. Samuel and his son therefore undertook to graft buds of this "red *criollo*" clone onto some of the trees in the plantation. They have now become experts in this very delicate technique of using an adult tree as stock for graft."

Consistent with his ideas, Samuel will not graft all his trees with this one clone.

Firstly, two others which seem just as promising have been selected on his land by Orlando, not to mention those deemed equally worthwhile on his neighbours' lands. Secondly, and much more fundamentally, the aim of this programme is to enhance the genetic diversity of a population of indigenous trees. And only choosing one clone would be tantamount to losing this diversity.

There remained the crucial phase: the tasting. For this, Samuel took us to his house. Guarded by a few large and initially rather terrifying dogs, a few dozen kilos of beans were drying on the concrete, beside the family's washing. I only had to bite into a single seed to realize that this cocoa had a remarkably long-lasting taste, without excessive bitterness. It seemed almost sweet. It was then that I had the idea of using the beans as they were, slightly crushed, that is, in the form of groats. To give them more character, I smoked them, using the skins of the seeds as fuel.

And so the red *criollo* chocolate known as Samuel was born, in homage to a determined planter.

« Samuel currently sells most of the cocoa he produces on the Mexican market. Its quality and its lingering taste are of great interest to a chocolate maker.

Homage to
an unknown inventor

*"El mole, como casi todas
las cosas esenciales, ya estaba
inventado cuando lo inventaron."*

Paco Ignacio Taibo I, *El libro de todos los moles*, 2003

Mole, a chocolate-based sauce served with chicken, is a symbol of the cookery of Puebla.

Among the gastronomic attractions that any self-respecting guide to Mexico City will recommend to visitors, the Café de Tacuba is certain to figure. Situated close to the city's great theatre, and still occupying the same premises as when it was founded in 1912 – the ground floor of a colonial-style building at N° 28 on the street of the same name – the Café de Tacuba claims to uphold the great tradition of Mexican cooking. The atmosphere is very pleasant, with its ceramic lower walls, its portrait gallery and its high vaulted ceilings, and the waitresses, looking like maids in their white lace uniforms, add to the timeless quality. The whole place is a true twentieth-century classic.

As befits the restaurant's status as a tourist attraction, the menu is written in several languages. But the place attracts a large local clientele, predominantly middle-class, who flock there all day long for churros, a *chocolate Tacuba* – the hot chocolate of the house – corn tamales, including sweet tamales, and guacamole, as well as dishes with a somewhat less local flavour, such as club sandwiches or curried chicken with rice.

One of my favourite tables is to the right of the entrance, facing the cash desk. From here, there is a perfect view of the whole length of the dining room and, above all, of a large mural showing ten nuns in the kitchen of their convent. This kitchen really exists, and is situated in the

« The Café de Tacuba, in the centre of Mexico City, is a meeting place for those seeking sophisticated local cooking.

As this painting illustrates, legend claims that the famous chocolate-based sauce was invented in a convent in Puebla (right, the city's Baroque cathedral).

city of Puebla, at 1205 Calle Tres Norte. It is richly decorated in ceramic tiles: the Talavera tiles common at that period in Mexico.

In this painting, a kneeling Indian woman is making tortillas by hand, apparently rolling out the dough on a *metate*. In accordance with the age-old cliché, it is the fattest of all the nuns who is serving the others – and what she is serving, from a large terracotta container, is a stew. To make it easier for us to identify this dish, the painter has placed in the centre of the picture, on one of the plates already served, a chicken drumstick.

In the bottom right-hand corner is a box explaining that the scene depicts the Dominican convent of Santa Rosa, where, according to legend, Sister Andrea de la Asunción invented the recipe for mole poblano, surely the most representative

symbol of Mexican tradition. Mole poblano is in fact a feature of the menu at the Café de Tacuba, where it is served in its most generic version, with chicken.

To really appreciate this chicken and its sauce, it is obvious that we must go to where this scene took place, where this drama was played out, in other words, to the city of Puebla de los Ángeles. Founded in 1531, Puebla occupies a strategic position on the map of Mexico, being halfway between the capital and the port of Veracruz. But it is best known to lovers of history and architecture for its impressive baroque cathedral and its reputation as one of the jewels of the Mexican baroque. It is even said that the spirit of Puebla cannot be understood without reference to this love of the baroque.

More prosaically, Puebla is considered to be the city where the traditions of

A chapel dedicated to the Virgin, peppers from Puebla and a tortilla: all the colours of Mexico at a glance.

Mexican cooking have been most lovingly preserved. And those who subscribe to this theory can point to a perfect example: mole poblano. This mole, which takes the form of a sauce made from ground or crushed ingredients, can be related to other great recipes which use the same procedure, like Genoese pesto or Indian curry.

Although there is no need for comparisons to justify its prestigious position in the world's culinary heritage, mole poblano does indeed closely resemble these two cousins, having the consistency of pesto, due to the use of fresh produce, and containing a veritable checklist of herbs and spices, like every curry or colombo in the world.

Nevertheless, none of these ingredients would have given this mole the aura which

surrounds it and which arouses such heated debate as to its origins if chocolate had not been added to the ingredients. The fact is that no one knows for sure where and how this brilliant invention came about. It will have to be a clever person indeed who one day manages to disentangle the reality from the myth.

An unquestioned authority on the subject, and one frequently quoted in the literature on chocolate, is Paco Ignacio Taibo I. Mixing fact and fiction, personal opinions and historical references, this novelist, born in Spain but resident in Mexico since 1958, has written several works devoted to his passion for food, including two on mole. The more recent of the two, *El libro de todos los moles*, published in 2003, develops and complements the first, *El Breviario del mole*

poblano, which appeared in 1981.

Taibo is not the only writer to have celebrated this culinary masterpiece in his work. In 1944, Rafael Helidoro Valle published an essay entitled *Anales del mole de guajolote*, in which he traces, with equal enthusiasm, the indigenous origins of turkey and the introduction of mole. Both these authors point out that *mole* derives from *mulli*, a Nahuatl word which the dictionary of Brother Alonso de Molina translates as *stew*.

Given the Nahuatl (and therefore partly Aztec) roots of the word, it might be supposed that the basic recipe for mole poblano dates back to pre-Colombian times.

This idea is rejected by both Taibo and Valle. Before the arrival of the Spanish, cocoa was only used for making drinks. It is not even certain that chocolate was first used for cooking in the New World. The earliest surviving written reference to the use of solid chocolate in a recipe dates from 1736 and takes the form of a verse diatribe called *Il Cioccolato*, written by the Italian poet Francesco Arisi, in which the author mentions, among other things, the use of chocolate in a sauce and in a recipe for polenta.

From corn polenta to Mexican tortillas is but a small step, and it is Paco Ignacio Taibo I who leads us there. In *El libro de todos los moles*, Taibo touches on two quite similar hypotheses, both claiming that what was to be mole poblano was invented by nuns in honour of an important figure of the period. According to some, this illustrious person was a bishop by the name of Don Juan Manuel Fernández de Santa Cruz y Sahagún, and the nuns in question were the Dominicans of

In one of the covered markets of Puebla, popular restaurants and grocers offer the local *mole*. »

Mole Poblano

Mixiote de Carnero
Caldo de Camarón
Coctel de Camarón

Comida Tipica Poblana
Caldo de Pollo
Pozole

Santa Rosa de Lima. Taibo dismisses this scenario for purely chronological reasons: in reality, the worthy prelate died nearly forty years before the convent was even founded.

The other hypothesis is that one of these nuns, Sister Andrea de la Asunción, invented a new dish to tickle the tastebuds of the Viceroy of New Spain, the Marqués de la Laguna, during one of his visits to Puebla. Once again, Taibo puts these events in a historical perspective: "Arriving in New Spain on November 7, 1680, the Marqués de la Laguna remained there until November 16, 1686" – at which time, the convent of Santa Rosa and its magnificent kitchen with the Talavera tiles had not yet been built. The nuns occupied a modest building and the rule of their convent was a strict one, which left little time for culinary invention.

Faced with such disappointment, Paco Ignacio Taibo I concludes with these magisterial words: 'Mole (poblano) was born without pomp. Like almost all essential things, it had already been invented when it was invented.'

How to resolve this deadlock? We may well suppose, for example, that mole poblano evolved from earlier preparations used in popular cookery, such as the simple porridge made by the peasants from corn tortilla, water and peppers, which they mashed up with the aid of a wooden pestle.

Dried chili peppers are in fact one of the basic, inescapable ingredients of mole poblano.

As for the addition of chocolate, it seems to be one of a number of such initiatives introduced by cooks over the centuries. The Spanish discovered what became chocolate in the form of a mixture used to make drinks that the Aztecs claimed had aphrodisiac properties, and all the experts agree that the conquistadors were particularly tantalized by the idea of increasing their sexual powers.

This one quality was enough to give rise to the habit of adding products derived from cocoa beans to everyday dishes.

How do things stand today in Puebla, home of the famous mole poblano?

As is common in popular cookery, each family, each restaurant has its own version of the recipe. In search of the best of these versions, I visited a restaurant named Mural de los Poblanos. The reason for the name becomes clear on seeing the huge fresco covering one of the walls of the dining room, depicting important figures from the city's past and present gathered together in a cheerfully anachronistic family portrait.

As for the object of my visit, the chef of the Mural de los Poblanos, Gabriela Guzmán Espinosa, was kind enough to list for me all the ingredients of her mole. The biggest surprise was that the tortilla is treated with a blowtorch until it is burned to a crisp before being added to the mixture.

The other ingredients, apart from chocolate, are small biscuits, raisins, almonds, peanuts, sesame seeds, aniseed, cinnamon, coriander, onion, garlic, plantains – and, of course, two varieties of chili pepper: *mulato* and *pasilla*. To achieve the consistency of a sauce, the mixture is thinned down with chicken stock.

In accordance with the modern tradition, Gabriela serves her mole at the Mural de los Poblanos with chicken and white rice. The mole is poured over the chicken, and the whole thing is sprinkled with sesame seeds. The original use of turkey instead of chicken seems to be a thing of the past.

But the proof of the pudding is always in the eating, and this mole was one of the best I have ever had the privilege to taste. Not all gastronomic discoveries are as comforting, though. As a starter, the waiter had recommended *escamoles* – a local caviar, he explained. It was rather white in colour, with a pleasant, slightly sweet taste. I discovered only later that this caviar is made from ants. Unwittingly, I had eaten ant larvae gathered from the roots of the agave.

My quest for mole, its origins and the most authentic recipe was not yet over. To be clear in my own mind, I needed to consult a specialist: Patricia Quintana, one of the greatest Mexican chefs and the author of a superb book with the highly appropriate title of *Náhuatl Mulli*.

Her mole poblano differs in several ways. She does not use biscuits, but adds dried cherries, sugar, tomatoes, tomatillos (*physalis*), and two other varieties of chili pepper: *ancho* and *chipotle*.

Reading this list, the thing that struck me was that many of the ingredients of this traditional recipe – cherries, tomatoes, raisins, plantains, garlic and cinnamon, to name a few – are not Mexican, or even Central American.

The Caribbean, the Mediterranean basin and Asia have all contributed flavours to those who have perfected mole poblano over the generations.

Cookery establishes its pedigree through cultural exchange, borrowing and assimilation.

Every restaurant, every family, has its own recipe for *mole poblano*, using at least two dozen different ingredients, **»** but the Mural de los Poblanos (with its painting of local personalities) certainly has one of the tastiest.

HOTEL

Chocolate

CHOCOLATE La Soledad

CHOCOLATE Y MOLE
La Soledad

La Soledad.

La Soledad.

The street
of chocolate

« On est convenu d'appeler chocolat
le mélange qui résulte de l'amande de cacao
grillée avec le sucre et la cannelle. »

Brillat-Savarin, *La Physiologie du goût*, 1825

Oaxaca has developed a very unusual tradition, unique of its kind: making chocolate mixtures to order, using cinnamon, almonds and unfermented cocoa beans as basic ingredients.

Few cities can pride themselves on having a traditional festival whose very name embodies the notion of a gift. In Zapotec, one of the regional languages, this festival is called Guelaguetza. *La Guelaguetza del Lunes del Cerro* – to give it its full name – symbolizes the offering made by the three regions surrounding Oaxaca to the city itself. On the two "Mondays of the Hill" following July 16, colourful crowds flock to Oaxaca for the impressive festivities.

The figure seven must have a particular significance in Oaxaca (pronounced *wa-ha-ka*), since it is also called the city of the seven moles, the most famous of which is *mole negro oaxaqueño*. Like its cousin from Puebla, this was originally an accompaniment to turkey. The mole made in Oaxaca uses a large number of ingredients, including some not found in *mole poblano*, such as marrow seeds, apple or pineapple.

Apart from its moles, Oaxaca claims a gastronomic tradition stretching back to the distant past. It is said that the region was the first to cultivate corn, which is used here to make a drink called *atole*, a mixture of corn and cocoa. Another local drink is *café de olla*: coffee boiled in a clay pot and spiced with cinnamon.

Those who appreciate the good things in life will certainly find what they are looking for in Oaxaca. The countryside around the city is full of bare hills on which a particular kind of agave grows in vast quantities. *Agave falcata var. espadina*, to give it its correct name, is the basic ingredient of mezcal, the famous traditional variant of tequila. (The tequila produced in other parts of Mexico is made from a different kind of agave.) Several million litres of mezcal – the total

national output – are distilled in four villages some fifty kilometres south of Oaxaca, the largest being Santiago Matatlán. You can't miss this village as you drive along Route MEX 190 from the south, and there is a strong incentive to stop there and drink yourself stupid in the warehouses of a local distiller.

Now imagine that, like me, you have learned to roll your Rs and pronounce the word *wa-ha-ka* like a native. You enter the city, pass the zocalo – the main square – and walk about three blocks to Calle Mina. Take the time to stop and look at every building along the way: since 1987, the historic centre has been designated a world heritage site.

When you get to Calle Mina, look for the corner of Calle 20 de Noviembre. You will see a sign saying *Chocolate Mayordomo*. If you are a lover of chocolate, you will know that you have reached the heart of the matter.

Almost directly opposite, on the white façade of a colonial-style building, is a large sign with the words *Chocolate La Soledad*, named after the Virgen de la Soledad, to whom the basilica of Oaxaca is dedicated. At eye level, your attention is drawn to an inscription: *Mejor chocolate, festival internacional del chocolate, Montbeliard, Francia.*

To complete the picture, you must walk a few metres along Calle 20 de Noviembre. There, Maria Teresa Núñez de Gómez waits behind the counter of her establishment. Maria Teresa is proud to be have been in at the beginning of an activity that has spread through the city like wildfire. In 1957, her husband Hector started grinding cocoa to make chocolate for the delectation of their customers. In 1962,

MEJOR CHOCOLATE

FESTIVAL INTERNACIONAL DEL CHOCOLATE MONTBELIARD, FRANCIA

La Soledad

the couple started a small business, which they named Guelaguetza!

Ever since, this business has been selling chocolate and mole specialities. Their initiative has been widely copied: today, there are more than a hundred small chocolate factories all over Oaxaca.

In the main room of Guelaguetza, which is predominantly blue, there is a row of machines, also painted blue. These are the grinders, which have clearly replaced the traditional *metate*. "We devised this system at the end of the 1950s," Maria Teresa explained. "The consumption of *cacao lavado* in the form of a drink is widespread in the region. It's the perfect high-energy drink. Our original idea was to provide an alternative that would save people the long and difficult process of making chocolate at home."

While Maria Teresa was explaining the birth of the family business, a short, elderly man came into the room, wearing a beige dust coat and a blue cap bearing the company's emblem. It was almost as if he had stepped out of the walls. In a way, he had. His name was Leon Pedro Cortez Zaccarias, and there was nothing he did not know about the workings of this battery of mechanical grinders. "We had the idea of adapting existing models, used to grind corn into flour, by having stones cut that were capable of grinding cocoa beans, which have a high fat content. We were already specialising in the roasting of beans. So this was simply a way of taking the transformation of the product one stage further."

Maria Teresa took up the story: "As with coffee, you have to find the ideal level of roasting. The roasted beans are then mixed, in the proportions requested

by the customer, with unshelled almonds and sticks of cinnamon. In Oaxaca, those are the only two ingredients we add for flavour. We don't use, for example, vanilla or *zapote*, let alone *achiote*. Even though every one of our customers has his own recipe, there isn't much variation in the proportion of cinnamon to beans or almonds to beans. The amount of sugar used, on the other hand, varies a lot. On average, we are asked for two kilos of sugar for every kilo of beans. Those who prefer a more bitter chocolate use only one kilo of sugar. At the other extreme, we are sometimes asked for four kilos of sugar for one kilo of cocoa!"

With an almost disturbing mechanical noise, the old machines were set in motion. Leon Pedro first poured the crystallised sugar into the hopper, presumably to remove the fat from the grindstones. Next came the contents of a tray corre-sponding to the customer's order. With the aid of a wooden tool, Leon pushed the beans, the sticks of cinnamon bark and the almonds into the grinder, from which an almost liquid paste was squeezed out. It only remained then to mix in the sugar and put the whole mixture through another grinder.

Leaving Guelaguetza with my precious Oaxaca chocolate, I felt duty bound to sample the atmosphere of a Mayordomo shop. This more recently established brand has been a great success, thanks to clever marketing. According to the young, smiling female assistants, there are now fifteen branches in the city and the brand's success shows no signs of abating.

The question remains as to why Oaxaca has remained the only city in Mexico where this remarkable tradition flour-ishes. But that's another story!

Dominique Persoone in Guelaguetza, the shop where made-to-order chocolate was first introduced to Oaxaca, with »
Pedro, who has worked for María Teresa Núñez de Gómez since the business was founded. Following pages: with its fifteen branches, Mayordomo is by far the most dynamic company in the area.

Chocolate at last

« *Avoir, sentir la matière première dans les mains, celle qui vient de la terre, et la transformer en chocolat.* »

Mathieu Brees, 2008

Mathieu Brees, who has had a passion for cocoa since he was twelve, has realized his dream by opening a Belgian chocolate shop in Mérida. He spends a good deal of his time seeking out the best cocoa pods on the plantations of Tabasco and Chiapas.

It is hard to believe, when you meet Mathieu Brees, that when he was in short trousers his classmates called him Fatty. And yet, even today, he is one of those who encourage us to commit the sin of gluttony. (Is it really a sin? That's another matter.)

Mathieu is a Belgian, and his nationality is highly significant. He was born in the south of Belgium, in the landscape of forests and fields known as Gaume, on the borders of France and Luxembourg. It was there that he developed that love of nature which has never left him. Mathieu also has something of a taste for adventure, and has found a perfect way to satisfy it: cocoa.

Mathieu was twelve years old when he first saw a demonstration by a chocolate maker. It left him fascinated. But it was not yet time to embark on a career in confectionery. His parents were determined that he receive a normal education, leading to university.

He was fifteen when an even more decisive encounter took place. She too was Belgian and her name was Stéphanie. The two teenagers did not know it yet, but this was the beginning of their adventure.

Having graduated from high school, Mathieu was finally able to do what he wanted. He enrolled in catering school, to learn confectionery and chocolate making. His first in-house training was at a famous restaurant, Le Clos Saint-Denis, awarded two stars in the Michelin guide. From the great chefs Mathieu learned things he has come to prize above all else: a feeling for detail, a perfectionism.

Mathieu was twenty. So was Stéphanie. They pooled their savings and took their first vacation: a tour of the Amazon jungle of Venezuela. The impact was enormous. Walking in that wild nature became a drug. The animals were incredible. Mathieu saw the first cocoa trees of his life – wild ones, to boot. He had discovered his obsession.

Stéphanie finished her course in hotel management. In the summer of 2001, no sooner were her exams over than she and Mathieu set off back to Venezuela with a one-way ticket and 2,500 euros in their pockets. These funds soon ran out, and the jobs they had been promised on Isla Margarita fell through. September 11 2001 had just happened, and was having a devastating effect on the hotel industry.

Without knowing it, Mathieu had an escape route in his pocket, in the form of the business card of a man named Jim Celis, a freelance engineer specializing in the installation of turbines. This stranger must have been friendly or generous, or probably both: having just bought a car from Mathieu's uncle, he had listened to him talking about his nephew, about whom he was very worried, and when he heard about the young man's ambitions, he had spontaneously given Mathieu's uncle his business card.

In desperation, Mathieu decided to call Jim, who invited him to a barbecue he was having with some friends. Stéphanie and he bought a plane ticket, which cost them half of their remaining savings. Flying over the Caribbean and the jungle in a Cessna was to remain an indelible memory for both of them.

When they arrived in Maturín, on the banks of the Orinoco, where Jim lived, they went to a supermarket and bought what they needed to make some little bags of chocolates. They even found a few

From Venezuela, where Mathieu and his wife Stéphanie began their career in Latin America, they moved to Yucatán, **»** a region known for its old colonial *haciendas*.

Cacao Uranga

Cacao Blanco Marfil

bars of Côte d'Or chocolate. In their hotel room, Mathieu made a ganache and its coating, Stéphanie wrapped the results of this improvised creation, and now they had some surprise gifts for the guests at the barbecue.

Jim, their guardian angel, realized that he had to put the young couple in contact with potential employers. The manager of the Hotel Stauffer sent for them the very next day. Mathieu became head pastry cook. Six months later, the barbecue produced another result. Ludo Gillis, a Belgian chocolate maker who owned a workshop called La Praline in Caracas, needed to find a replacement for his head

of production, who had left for pastures new. He hired Mathieu, who discovered traditional methods of chocolate manufacture, such as were practised a hundred years ago. "We made everything from natural materials. For a nut-filled chocolate, for example, Ludo used nuts from Amazonia." To have, to feel, the raw material in your hands, straight from the earth, and to transform it into chocolate, became a necessity.

Caracas in those years was not the safest of places. When eleven people were murdered in their neighbourhood, Stéphanie had had enough. The couple decided to take a few days' vacation in Yucatán. Jim and his wife Hilda, who was born in Campeche, were full of enthusiasm for this region of Mexico, probably the safest in the country – and a place where cocoa was produced!

Thinking of moving there in the future, Mathieu made a list of what he had been offered by way of chocolate. Stéphanie wasted no time. Within three days, she had found a house which could accommodate a small chocolate workshop, and bought it. Six months later, in July 2003, their chocolate shop L'Amandine opened on Calle 5D in the Pensiones district of Mérida.

Mathieu had a valuable ally: the reputation of Belgian chocolates. But his intention was to use only Mexican cocoas. In Tabasco, he hoped to find the right product and the right quality. He met Vicente Gutiérrez Cacep, whose *hacienda* was equipped with an assembly line for transforming cocoa.

Vicente, who understood the young Belgian's vision, placed his knowledge at his disposal.

Mathieu has developed new mixtures of beans, as well as hints of aroma in his chocolates. He wraps – in both a literal and a figurative sense – the secrets of their manufacture and their incredible vanilla fragrance in big pastilles of cocoa butter.

The story of an entrepreneur often begins with modest facilities, which increase as more money is invested. The workshop also has to evolve and sometimes needs to be enlarged. Mathieu has already been through these stages.

If you want to be one of the big boys, making good chocolate from sugar and cocoa beans requires two important operations. They are both performed by a machine called a conche. Firstly, it is essential to make sure that the beans are ground as finely as possible and to take the time to do it. Secondly, the mass must be heated in such a way that the volatile fatty acids with their unpleasant taste evaporate.

What else is there to do when you are living for your passion and the cocoa beans you need grow in the country you have made your own? The answer is obvious. You must scour the countryside until you find original beans and, just as importantly, men and women capable of developing the potential of those beans in the course of fermentation. Every other weekend, the little Ford Fiesta sets off for the states of Tabasco and Chiapas, covering 2,000 kilometres each time.

It was in the course of one of these exploratory trips that Mathieu met Tito's daughter Mónica, who had just completed a course on the transformation of cocoa. She revealed to him the treasures of the *rancho* La Concepción, and the *uranga*, the *blanco marfil* and the *ceylan* have now become bars of dark chocolate, with a brand name that is already starting to become well known: *Ki'xocolatl*. An amusing linguistic detail is that this name mixes Nahuatl and Maya, *ki* meaning *good* in the Maya of Yucatán.

And so this expedition to Mexico comes to an end, biting at last into a bar of "clonal" chocolate. And what chocolate!

Recipes

Spread

FOR 350G OF SPREAD:
1 pod of frosted Madagascan vanilla,
100g of fresh cream (40% fat content),
100g of glucose or 100g of acacia honey,
100g of Peru 64 dark chocolate,
50g of salted butter

Split the vanilla pod in 2 and scrape away the seeds using the blade of a knife.

Add the vanilla seeds and pod into the cream and bring to the boil.

Remove the vanilla pod and add the glucose.

Gently mix and pour over the chocolate (previously broken into small pieces). Stir the mixture until the chocolate is completely melted.

Cut the butter into small pieces and add to the chocolate paste. Mix to an even consistency.

Pour this into a glass or jar and leave to set at room temperature. Seal the container and keep refrigerated.

Mexican praliné

FOR 120 CHOCOLATES:
300g of macadamia nuts, 60g of water,
100g of caster sugar, 80g of brown sugar,
1.2g of powdered ancho peppers, 4g of
crushed coriander seeds, 120g of Papua
New Guinea 64 dark chocolate, 1g of sea salt
For the mould:
Papua New Guinea 64 dark chocolate
Mould cw 1561

Roast the macadamia nuts in the oven for 15 minutes at 160°C.

Prepare a syrup by pouring water into a copper pot, then adding the caster sugar and brown sugar. Cook until you obtain a caramel.

Add the hot nuts and spices (ancho pepper, coriander and sea salt) into the caramel. Mix well using a spatula. Keep stirring until the caramel takes on a sandy texture. This occurs when the caramel syrup crystallizes. Mix well. The sugar crystals will melt again and form a delicious caramel.

Pour the mixture onto baking parchment and leave to cool.

Coarsely grind it using either a blender or grinding machine. Do not grind for too long. The mechanical movements heat the nuts which then release their oil. The result is a greasy mixture.

Leave the praliné to briefly cool at room temperature. Mix it with the 120g of tempered Papua New Guinea 64 dark chocolate.

Mould the shapes with tempered fondant chocolate (Moulding, p.249).

Fill the praliné shapes, leave to harden, then cover over with tempered dark chocolate. Remove from mould after crystallisation.

Marmalade square

FOR A TRAY OF 60CM X 40CM:
For the bitter orange marmalade:
peel of 4 organic bitter "Valencia" oranges,
300g of "Valencia" orange juice,
3g of agar-agar, 300g of gelling sugar
For the baking:
egg wash (2 egg yolks, 5cl of water, salt),
140g of unsalted butter, 100g of bitter ganache
for the finishing (Spread recipe, p.190)
For the puff pastry: p.250

To make the bitter orange marmalade, rinse the 4 oranges and wipe dry. Grate a thin layer of peel. Using a whisk, mix together the agar-agar and the 300g of juice (already boiled). Add the grated peel and gelling sugar, then thicken (leave to reduce). Refrigerate the marmalade.

Cut a sheet of pastry into two equal parts and roll out again until it covers an area 40cm x 60cm. Place this onto a baking tray covered with baking parchment and pierce with a fork (to prevent the pastry from rising during baking).

Using a palette knife, spread a layer of marmalade – as thin as possible – over the pastry (during baking, the marmalade will produce a delicious caramel flavour).

Using a pastry wheel, cut strips of different widths, between 0.5 and 1cm, in a sheet of pastry that has not been rolled out, i.e. 0.5cm thick.

Place these strips diagonally 1cm apart onto the marmalade, then allow to rest in the refrigerator.

For the egg wash, beat the egg yolks, 5cl of water and a pinch of salt until you get a light mixture.

Brush egg wash over the square.

Pre-heat a hot air oven to 175°C, lightly glaze the square and bake for 15 minutes.

Melt 140g of butter in a saucepan and spread over the square (this will give it a mouth-watering butter flavour!).

Turn the square 180° for an all-over bake. Bake for another 15 minutes.

Melt the remainder of the marmalade on a low heat. When the square is baked through, brush marmalade over.

Leave to crisp up.

The square can also be covered with a freshly made bitter ganache. Place on a grill and cover with the ganache before it sets. Leave to crisp up.

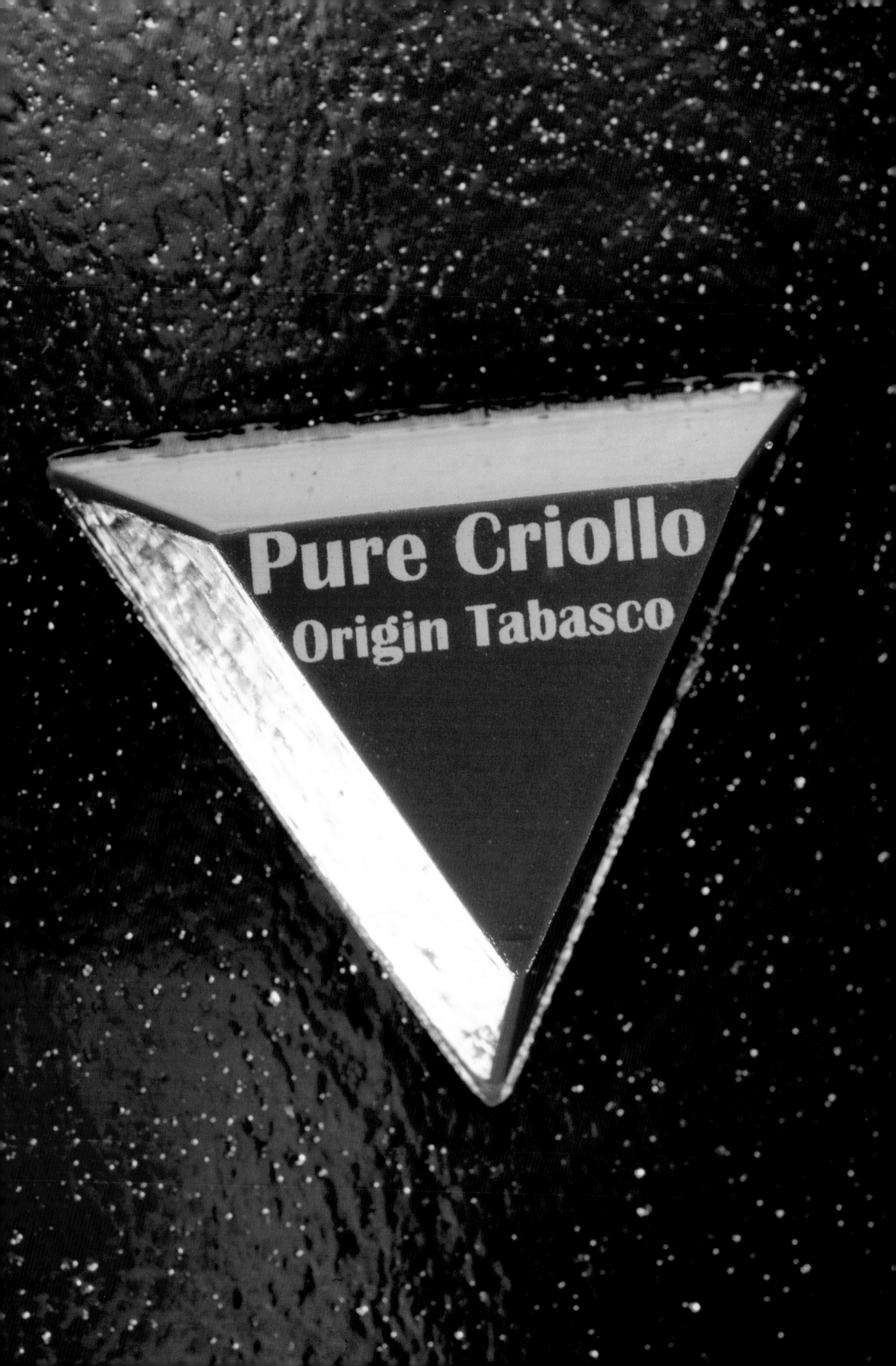
Pure Criollo
Origin Tabasco

Pure criollo origin "Tabasco"

FOR 58 CHOCOLATES:
560g of Tabasco 44 milk chocolate,
260g of fresh cream (40% fat content),
20g of glucose, 20g of invert sugar syrup
For the mould:
Tabasco 44 milk chocolate
Mould 1000 L11
Customised transfer sheets
"Pure Criollo, Origin Tabasco"

Place the transfer sheet between the mould and stainless steel lid, such that you can print (by transfer) the design onto the top face of the praline.
Temper the milk chocolate at 30–31°C and mould the shapes (Moulding, p.249).
To make the ganache, cut the chocolate into small pieces. Bring the cream to the boil and add (away from the heat) the glucose and invert sugar. Gently mix. Pour this hot cream over the chocolate and mix until all pieces melt.
At room temperature, leave the ganache to cool to 25–26°C. Fill the shapes with the ganache while still in liquid form.
Leave to harden for 2 hours at room temperature.
Cover in tempered Tabasco milk chocolate.
Leave the chocolate to crystallize.
Carefully remove from the mould, ensuring the transfer works properly.

Because Tabasco 44 milk chocolate is so rich in taste, it is important to retain its natural flavour as much as possible.

Mole poblano

FOR 50 CHOCOLATES:
20g of mole sauce, 10g of sesame seeds,
20g of browned chicken skin, 200g of peanut
praliné, 60g of Vanuatu 44 milk chocolate
For the mole sauce:
100g of crushed almonds, 3 dried mulato peppers,
2 dried pasilla peppers, 1g of salt, 50g of sesame
seeds, 1.5g of anise seeds, 1 garlic clove,
1/2 a roasted tortilla, 1.5g of coriander seeds,
1.5g of crushed clove, 60g of bitter dark chocolate
For the mould:
Peru 64 dark chocolate
Mould cw 1565

To make the mole sauce, pour all the ingredients – except the chocolate – into a blender or shredder bowl. Once you get a fairly fine granular texture, add the melted chocolate (40°C) and mix to an even consistency.

Brown the sesame seeds in a pan, without using fat. Stir well and remove immediately to prevent overcooking.

Place in the refrigerator.

Mould the square shapes with tempered Peru 64 chocolate (Moulding, p.249).

Remove the skin of a large corn-fed chicken. Cook it medium rare in salted water.

Start the cooking from cold. Bring to the boil and leave to simmer for 15 to 25 minutes, depending on the quality of the skin.

Drain the skin then dry with absorbent paper.

Fry the skin in oil at 180°C until it turns crispy and all traces of moisture have disappeared.

Drain the chicken skin chips on absorbent paper and cut into small pieces.

Mix the praliné with tempered milk chocolate, add the chips, sesame seeds and mole paste, and gently mix together.

Cover the slices with praliné chocolate fondant (± 2 to 3 mm thick) to produce a thin biscuit.

Leave to harden for 15 minutes at room temperature.

Looped mendiants

FOR 50 CHOCOLATES:
250g of your preferred chocolate
For milk and dark chocolate:
popcorn, cocoa beans, Maldon salt flakes
For a white and dark chocolate blend:
mango confit, papaya confit, star anise,
roasted sesame seeds
For a milk and white chocolate blend:
pineapple confit, whole nutmeg, cumin seeds,
roasted Macadamia nuts, angelica confit
Short sticks for skewers 18cm long (e.g. bamboo)

To create shiny fruits and nuts, lay some rigid plastic sheets (acetate type) onto a work surface. Line up the sticks ± 8cm from each other.

Temper the chocolate(s) chosen then create intertwining loops using a cone.

Before they completely harden (be careful, this happen fast!), garnish with ingredients of your choice.

Leave the chocolate to solidify at room temperature, then carefully detach from the plastic. The sheets can be washed for immediate re-use.

For the presentation, it is best to use a base that the sticks can be inserted into: a bowl or glass filled with sesame seeds, rice or salt.

Guacamole

FOR 60 CHOCOLATES:
125g of fresh cream (40% fat content), 1g of fresh garlic, 10g of glucose, 2.5g of fresh coriander leaves, 125g of Blanc Intense white chocolate, 60g of ripe avocado flesh, 6g of lemon juice, 1.6g of tomato purée, 0.8g of chilli powder (Xcatic chilli), 10g of tequila, 60g of hazelnut praliné (50/50), 20g of Belcolade hazelnut paste BF-HP1, 40g of milk chocolate, 16g of tortilla chips

For the colouring:
50g of Blanc Intense white chocolate, 25g of cocoa butter, 2g of yellow colouring powder, 2g of green colouring powder

For the mould:
Blanc Intense white chocolate
Mould cw 1573

Prepare a mixture of 2/3 dark chocolate and 1/3 cocoa butter. Melt the mixture at 40°C in a microwave oven (at 350W). Add the colourings and gently mix.
Stir until the colouring is evenly spread throughout the mixture. Sieve the mixture, then cool to 31°C.
Using an airbrush, spray a thin layer of the mixture into the mould. Leave to crystallize at room temperature.
Cover the mould with a layer of tempered white chocolate (28–29°C) (Moulding, p.249).
Bring the cream to the boil with the garlic clove (germ already removed).
Add the glucose and coriander and mix through.
Cut the white chocolate into thin pieces. Pour the hot cream over these. Gently mix until all bits of chocolate have melted.
Mix the avocado flesh and lemon juice together.
Add this purée to the mixture.
Pour in the tomato purée, 0.2g of chilli powder and the tequila. Mix to a smooth, even consistency.
Leave the ganache to cool then fill one of the two pyramids, i.e. half the mould.
Mix together the hazelnut praliné, hazelnut paste and tempered milk chocolate. Break the tortilla chips into small pieces then add these in, along with the remainder of the chilli powder. Gently mix all ingredients together then fill the second pyramid with the ganache.
Leave to harden for 2 hours at room temperature, then cover the mould with tempered white chocolate.
Crystallize for 15 minutes at room temperature.
Remove pralines from the mould after complete crystallisation.

Licuado

FOR 45 CHOCOLATES:
100g of fresh cream (40% fat content),
0.1g of cinnamon, 1 clove, 0.3g of whole nutmeg,
1g of cardamom, 5g of dark brown sugar,
50g of ripe banana purée, 100g of Blanc
Intense white chocolate, 5g of lemon juice
For the colouring:
50g of Blanc Intense white chocolate, 25g of
cocoa butter, 4g of yellow colouring powder DC033
For the mould:
Blanc Intense white chocolate
Mould cw 1560

The night before, prepare a mixture of 2/3 white chocolate, 1/3 cocoa butter. Melt the mixture at 40°C. Add the colouring powder.

Mix together and ensure the colour spreads evenly through. Pour the mixture through a fine sieve and cool to 31°C.

Using an airbrush, spray a thin layer of the mixture into the mould.

Cover the mould with a layer of white chocolate tempered at 28–29°C (Moulding p.249).

Boil the cream together with the spices (cinnamon, clove, whole nutmeg and cardamom) and brown sugar. Cover with a plastic sheet then leave to infuse overnight in the refrigerator.

Bring the cream to the boil again and filter the spices. Add the banana purée and cook again.

Cut the Blanc Intense chocolate into small pieces and cover with the hot cream. Gently mix until all pieces of chocolate have melted.

Pour in the lemon juice and stir to a smooth consistency. Leave to cool.

Fill the moulds with the banana ganache. Leave to harden then cover the moulds in tempered white chocolate. Leave to crystallize for 15 minutes at room temperature.

Remove from the mould.

To keep the pralines for longer periods, add a drop (10g) of banana liqueur into the fresh cream.

Basil mango

FOR 60 CHOCOLATES:
150g of pure, ripe mango flesh, 20g of glucose,
2g of basil leaves, 5g of lemon juice,
peel of 1 organic lemon, 100g of
Peru 64 dark chocolate, 25g of butter
For the colouring:
50g of Blanc Intense white chocolate, 25g of
cocoa butter, 4g of orange colouring powder E110
For the mould:
Blanc Intense white chocolate
Mould cw 1559

Prepare a mixture of 2/3 white chocolate, 1/3 cocoa butter. Melt the mixture at 40°C.

Add the colouring powder.

Mix until the colours spread evenly through. Pour the mixture through a fine sieve and cool to 31°C.

Using an airbrush, spray a thin layer of the mixture into the mould.

Cover the mould with a layer of Blanc Intense white chocolate tempered at 28–29°C (Moulding, p.249).

Cut the mango flesh into large cubes. Add the glucose, basil leaves and lemon juice.

Grate a thin layer of the lemon skin and add in.

Reduce the mixture 3/4. Filter through a fine sieve.

Separate the dark chocolate into small pieces and cover over with the mixture. Gently mix until all pieces of chocolate have melted.

Cut up the butter and add in. Mix to a smooth, even consistency.

Leave the ganache to cool to 25–26°C (i.e. below 27°C), at room temperature. Fill the moulds while the ganache is still in liquid form.

Once it hardens, after about 2 hours at room temperature, cover the moulds with tempered white chocolate. Remove from the mould.

Bitter chocolate truffle

FOR 165 CHOCOLATES:
1kg of Papua New Guinea 64 dark chocolate,
1 Madagascar Bourbon vanilla pod, 450g of fresh
cream (40% fat content), 200g of salted butter,
300g of bitter cocoa powder, 150g of icing sugar

Cut 500g of chocolate into small pieces.

Split the vanilla pod in half and scrape out the seeds using the blade of a knife. Bring the cream to the boil with the seeds and split pod. Take out the pod and pour the hot cream over the chocolate. Mix until all pieces have melted.

Cut the butter into small pieces and add to the ganache to produce a smooth mixture.

Leave the mixture to cool at room temperature until creamy.

Using a piping bag, make small paste balls 2.5cm in diameter. Leave to harden in the refrigerator.

Mix the cocoa powder and icing sugar together then sieve (using a fine sieve).

Temper the 500g of remaining chocolate.

Using a two-pronged dipping fork, run the ganache balls through the tempered chocolate.

Remove any excess chocolate by gently shaking the fork up and down.

Roll the ganache balls through the cocoa powder and sugar mixture.

Leave to crystallize for 10 minutes at room temperature.

Carefully place the balls in a sieve (mesh: 0.5cm).

Gently shake to remove any excess cocoa powder.

Grand-mother's truffle

FOR 120 CHOCOLATES:
250g of salted butter, 100g of fondant,
25g of invert sugar, 75g of hazelnut praliné
(50/50), 2kg of Venezuela 43 milk chocolate

Use butter at room temperature. Place in a blender (fitted with a dasher) and mix to a light and creamy white texture.

Add the fondant and invert sugar (cut into small bits). Mix again to an even consistency.

Pour in the hazelnut praliné and mix.

Finish with 400g of tempered milk chocolate. Stir the mixture until smooth.

Using a piping bag with a round tube 1cm in diameter, create small identical balls 3cm in diameter on baking parchment.

Leave to harden for 30 minutes at 10°C.

Make some shavings using 800g of milk chocolate. To do this, spread tempered chocolate over a smooth surface (marble or stainless steel). The chocolate will partially crystallize after a few minutes. Using a triangular spatula, scrape thin shavings off the chocolate surface.

Place the shavings in a large, flat plastic container.

Temper the 800g of remaining milk chocolate.

Using a two-pronged dipping fork, run the ganache balls through the tempered chocolate.

Remove any excess chocolate by gently shaking the fork up and down.

Carefully roll the ganache balls through the chocolate shavings.

Leave to crystallize for 15 minutes at room temperature.

The shavings can be created using a more traditional method. Take a large kitchen knife and scrape over a sizeable piece of fairly hard chocolate to create tiny spirals.

Mexican gazpacho

FOR 100 CHOCOLATES:
65g of frozen orange purée, 65g of frozen pineapple purée, 65g of frozen mango purée, 200g of dark chocolate, 20g of glucose, peel of 1/2 a lime, juice of 1/2 a lime, 50g of butter, 2g of chilli powder (mulatto type), 200g of almond praliné (50/50), 40g of grated parmesan, 80g of milk chocolate
For the mould:
Peru 64 dark chocolate
Mould cw 1571

Cast the mould in tempered Peru chocolate and leave to set in the refrigerator (Moulding, p.249).

Mix the orange, pineapple and mango purées in a copper saucepan, adding in the glucose and lime juice. Grate a thin layer of lime peel and add into the mixture, together with 0.5g of chilli.

Heat the mixture until it gently simmers. Leave simmering until the mixture reduces by 1/3.

Cut the dark chocolate into small pieces. Slowly pour the hot fruit purée over these, turning regularly, until the chocolate is completely melted.

Leave to stand for 5 minutes.

Cut the butter into small pieces and add in. This will help produce a smooth mixture.

Refrigerate this ganache, then use it to fill the mould 2/3 the way up. Leave to set.

Mix the almond praliné together with tempered milk chocolate.

Add the parmesan and 1.5g of chilli powder, then mix gently.

Fill the remainder of the praliné mould.

Leave to crystallize and cover with tempered Peru 64 dark chocolate.

Remove from mould after complete crystallisation.

Samuel
red
criollo

FOR 20 CHOCOLATES:
10g of fermented criollo cocoa beans,
60g of dark hazelnut praliné (50/50),
20g of Belcolade hazelnut paste BF-HP1,
30g of Venezuela 43 milk chocolate
For the colouring:
50g of Peru 64 dark chocolate,
25g of cocoa butter,
4g of red powder colouring
For the mould:
Peru 64 dark chocolate
Mould cw 1563

Roast the cocoa beans for 25 minutes at 130°C. Leave to cool slightly then rub them to remove the thin outer layer. Place this to the side.

Put the beans into a plastic bag and attach to the chimney of an Aladin Instant Smoke Pipe.

Stoke with bits of the removed layer then light it. The bag soon fills up with smoke.

Seal the bag using adhesive tape, minimising any loss of smoke, and refrigerate for 12 hours. The beans will be smoked cold!

Prepare a mixture of 2/3 dark chocolate and 1/3 cocoa butter. Melt the mixture at 45°C in a microwave oven (at 350 W). Add the red colouring and gently mix. Stir until the colouring is evenly spread throughout the mixture. Sieve this, then cool at 31°C.

Using a cone, pipe a small amount of coloured chocolate into the bottom part of the moulds. Leave to set at room temperature then cast the shape in tempered dark chocolate (Moulding, p.249).

Open the plastic bag and break the beans using a rolling pin to obtain a crushed grué texture.

Mix together the hazelnut praliné, hazelnut paste and tempered milk chocolate.

Add the broken beans and thoroughly mix together. Fill the moulds with this mixture.

Leave to crystallize for 15 minutes then cover with tempered dark chocolate.

Remove from mould after complete crystallisation.

Achiote

FOR 60 CHOCOLATES:
100g of fresh orange juice, 20g of achiote seeds,
100g of fresh cream (40% fat content), 100g of
Blanc Intense white chocolate, 1g of organic
orange peel, 10g of glucose, 25g of butter,
60g of almond praliné, 20g of Venezuela 43
milk chocolate, 5g of cumin nougatine
For the mould:
dark chocolate 60%, Venezuela 43 milk chocolate
For the cumin nougatine:
10g of glucose, 100g of caster sugar,
5g of cumin seeds
Mould cw 1563

The night before, pour boiling orange juice over the achiote seeds. Transfer into a bowl, cover with cling film, then leave to soak for 12 hours in the refrigerator. Temper the dark chocolate at 31–32°C and the milk chocolate at 30°C. Using a cone, pour dark chocolate into the bottom part of the mould (a stylised mountain shape). Leave to crystallize.

Cover the mould with a layer of milk chocolate (Moulding, p.249).

To make the nougatine, melt the glucose in a copper saucepan. Gradually add the caster sugar until the crystals melt into the mixture. Mix well using a spatula. Colour the mixture with sugar until it turns light brown, then add the cumin seeds away from the heat. Gently mix together.

Pour the boiling mixture between 2 sheets of baking paper. Flatten out using a rolling pin until 2 mm thick. Leave the nougatine to cool.

Bring the cream to the boil. Break the white chocolate into small pieces. Filter the juice to remove the achiote seeds. Then add the juice, finely grated peel and cream glucose. Pour this hot mixture over the white chocolate and stir to an even consistency.

Cut the butter into small pieces and add to the mixture. Mix until the butter melts in.

Leave to cool, then fill the mould with a ganache 2/3 the way up.

Mix the almond praliné and the 20g of tempered milk chocolate.

Break the nougatine into small pieces and add in. Mix together and fill the mould to the top.

Leave to crystallize and cover with tempered Venezuela 43 milk chocolate.

Remove from mould after complete crystallisation.

Chili con carne

FOR 65 CHOCOLATES:
150g of red kidney beans, 125g of fondant, 5g of glucose, 125g of fresh cream (40% fat content), 30g of unsalted butter, 2.5g of browned onion, flour, neutral frying oil, 10g of smoked bacon, 0.2g of cumin seeds, 60g of hazelnut praliné (50/50), 20g of Belcolade hazelnut paste BF-HP1, 30g of milk chocolate, 0.6g of Espelette chilli powder, salt
For the mould:
Costa Rica 38 milk chocolate, Costa Rica 64 dark chocolate
Mould cw 1555

Temper the milk chocolate and dark chocolate. Colour the centre (top part) of the mould with the dark chocolate. Mould the remainder with milk chocolate. Leave to crystallize in the refrigerator (Moulding, p.249).

Rinse the red kidney beans in water. Soak in cold water and leave to swell for 12 hours in the refrigerator. Throw the beans into boiling water. Cook through for about 30 minutes. Carefully strain. Salt and mix into a purée, using a blender for example. Sieve to obtain a fine purée.

Make some caramel by combining fondant and glucose. Whisk the caramel with the boiling cream. Add the bean purée to the caramel. Cut the butter into small pieces and spread throughout the mixture. Leave to melt and mix in, then leave to cool.

Fill the mould half way up with the bean caramel. Leave to set.

Peel an onion then cut into very thin slices using a vegetable slicer or mandoline.

Separate the onion slices, cover in flour and sieve to remove any excess flour.

Fry the onion slices in oil at 180°C until crunchy and dry. Absorb any excess oil.

Place the smoked bacon slices between two sheets of absorbent paper. Dry them in a microwave oven until crispy like chips.

Brown the cumin seeds in a pan and grind to a fine powder.

Mix the hazelnut paste and the praliné with tempered milk chocolate.

Mix the bacon chips and fried onion rings together to obtain a gritty powder. Add this to the cumin seed powder and chilli powder. Add this powder mixture to the praliné just made. Gently mix.

Fill the other half of the mould with this praliné. Leave to harden for 15 minutes at room temperature. Cover the shape in tempered milk chocolate, then leave to crystallize at room temperature. Remove from the mould.

Jamaican flowers

FOR 160 CHOCOLATES:
210g of fresh cream (40% fat content), 15g of
dried Jamaican flowers (Hibiscus sabdariffa),
5g of fresh mint, 20g of glucose,
210g of milk chocolate
For the colouring:
25g of cocoa butter, 50g of dark chocolate,
4g of red powder colouring
For the mould:
Costa Rica 64 dark chocolate
Mould cw 1553

Prepare a mixture of 2/3 dark chocolate and 1/3 cocoa butter. Melt the mixture at 45°C in a microwave oven (at 350W). Add the red colouring and gently mix. Stir until the colouring is evenly spread throughout the mixture. Sieve this then cool at 31°C.

Using an airbrush, spray a thin layer of this mixture into the mould.

Temper the dark chocolate at 31–32°C then cover the mould with a layer of this. Leave to solidify at room temperature, then crystallize in a cool place (Moulding, p.249).

Bring the cream to the boil and add in the dried flowers and mint leaves. Leave to infuse for 1 hour. Re-heat this mixture then strain. Add the glucose and mix together away from the heat.

Break the milk chocolate into small pieces and cover with the hot mixture. Stir until all pieces are melted into the mixture.

Leave the ganache to cool then fill the moulds. Cover the mould with tempered Costa Rica dark chocolate. Wait until the ganache has solidified enough before removing from the mould. These two steps are to be carried out at room temperature.

Xcatic chilli

FOR 140 CHOCOLATES:
2.25g of Xcatic chilli powder
(or Espelette chilli), 100g of marzipan (50/50),
175g of fresh cream (40% fat content),
13g of Lapsang Souchong smoked tea,
12g of glucose, 375g of Tabasco 44 pure
criollo milk chocolate, 12g of invert sugar paste
For the mould:
Tabasco 44 pure criollo milk chocolate
Mould 1000 L15
Personalised transfer sheets
in the shape of chillis

Cut the Xcatic chilli in half, remove the seeds and crush it into a fine powder.

Place the personalised transfer sheet between the mould and stainless steel lid. This will enable you to print (by transfer) the design onto the top face of the praline.

Coat the mould with a layer of tempered milk chocolate (Moulding, p.249).

Mix the marzipan and chilli powder together. Roll this pastry out between two sheets of stiff plastic or baking parchment until 2mm thick.

Using a tear drop pastry cutter, make "tears" of chilli marzipan and place them in each mould individually. Bring the cream to the boil, add the tea, then leave to infuse for 10 minutes. Filter the cream through a fine sieve, pressing the tea with the underside of a soup spoon to squeeze the cream through. Add more cream if necessary until you have 175g.

Boil the cream again, this time adding glucose. Cut the chocolate into thin pieces and cover with this mixture. Add the invert sugar. Mix until the chocolate melts and you obtain a smooth, even consistency.

Cool the ganache at room temperature (to ± 26°C) and fill the moulds while the ganache is still in liquid form. Leave to harden at room temperature for about 2 hours. Cover the shapes again with tempered milk chocolate.

Remove from the mould.

The Xcatic chilli (a Mayan name) grows wildly in Yucatán, as does the habanero chilli which is more widely known. Espelette chilli is another option for this recipe.

Café de olla

FOR 35 CHOCOLATES:
100g of fresh cream (40% fat content),
100g of Costa Rica 38 milk chocolate, 10g of
glucose, 3g of cinnamon, 2 cloves, 5g of dark
brown sugar, 2g of organic orange peel,
10g of instant coffee, 35 small roasted
coffee grains, gold powder
For the mould:
Costa Rica 64 dark chocolate
Mould HA 10176

The night before, bring the cream to the boil with the cinnamon, cloves and sugar.
Cover with a plastic film and leave to soak overnight in the refrigerator.
Cover the mould – coffee cup shapes – with a layer of tempered dark chocolate (Moulding, p.249).
Filter the cream, then add the finely grated orange peel and instant coffee. Bring to the boil again. Mix well.
Cut the milk chocolate into small pieces and cover over with the cream. Mix until the chocolate melts in.
Add the glucose.
Leave the ganache to cool, ensuring it remains in liquid form.
Fill the coffee cups with the ganache.
Leave to crystallize and cover with tempered Costa Rica 64 dark chocolate.
Roll the coffee grains in gold powder. Use a sieve to remove any excess powder. Using tongs, place a golden grain on each cup.

UFO

FOR 72 CHOCOLATES:
250g of orange juice, 0.5g of agar-agar,
peel of 2 organic oranges, 125g of gelling
sugar, 215g of almond praliné (50/50),
85g of Venezuela 43 milk chocolate,
38g of caramelised coconut (p.251)
For the colouring:
200g of Blanc Intense white chocolate,
100g of cocoa butter, fat-soluble powder
colouring: 2g of blue powder colouring,
6g yellow powder colouring
For the mould:
Venezuela 43 milk chocolate
Mould cw 1552

Mix the white chocolate and cocoa butter together. Melt this at 40°C. Separate into 2 equal parts. Pour 4g of yellow colouring into one half. In the other half, pour 2g of yellow colouring and 2g of blue colouring. Gently mix each half separately until the colouring completely dissolves. Pour each coloured mixture through a fine sieve and temper (31°C).

A UFO mould is made up of two corresponding parts, representing the top and bottom parts of the eventual praline. Other colour combinations can also be used. To proceed, cover one of the halves of the mould with a fairly large piece of cardboard. Using an airbrush, spray green colouring on what will be the top part of the UFO. Turn the cardboard over and spray yellow colouring on what will be the bottom part of the UFO. Line the moulds with tempered milk chocolate (Moulding, p.249). Bring the orange juice to the boil and reduce by half, i.e. to 125g.

Grate the peel of the 2 oranges. Add the agar-agar, peel and gelling sugar into the juice.

Bring the marmalade to the boil and mix with a spatula to get a thick, even consistency. Leave to cool. Fill the top part of the UFOs (coloured green) with cold marmalade.

Mix together the almond praliné, tempered milk chocolate and bits of caramelised coconut. Fill the bottom part of the UFOs with this mixture.

Leave the praliné to harden for 15 minutes at room temperature.

Seal each part of the eventual pralines with tempered milk chocolate. Lightly scrape the surface to remove any excess chocolate.

Immediately join two shapes head-to-tail, such that the two parts (top and bottom) of what will be a dual-coloured UFO fit together perfectly.

Leave the pralines to harden at room temperature for 2 hours.

Remove from the mould.

Tequila marsh-mallows

FOR 60 CAKES:
600 g of biscuit mixture (p.251), 400g of hazelnut praliné, 180g of Costa Rica 38 milk chocolate, 340g of agave syrup, 340g of S2 caster sugar, 230g of water, 200g of egg whites, 13g of gelatine leaves, 56g of Silver tequila, white spirit vinegar (to remove fat from the bowl and beater)
For the coating:
Peru 64 dark chocolate,
a few Maldon salt granules

Using a pastry cutter (diameter: 4cm), cut out circles from the biscuit mixture and lay out on an oven-proof dish covered in baking parchment.

Pre-heat the oven to 170°C and bake the biscuits for 10 minutes.

Leave to cool. Keep in a metal container until they need to be used.

Mix the hazelnut praliné and tempered milk chocolate. Pour the mixture into a piping bag and spread a thin layer (± 5 mm) on each biscuit.

Use vinegar to remove the fat from the blender bowl and beater, then briskly beat the egg whites to a solid consistency.

Bring the agave syrup, sugar and water to the boil (115°C). Dribble this over the beaten egg whites and briskly beat again until it reaches a temperature of 35°C.

Wet the gelatine leaves in cold water. Wring dry and add to the above mixture together with the tequila. Beat again until the mixture starts to cool. Pour into a piping bag.

Fit the piping bag with a 2cm diameter round nozzle, and make small round towers 4cm high, roughly the same diameter as the biscuit. Leave to harden for 4 hours at room temperature.

Temper the dark chocolate. Dip the marshmallows into the chocolate, spongy side first, biscuit facing upwards. Using a dipping-fork, dip the biscuit in from the bottom up, such that the top comes out of the chocolate first. Repeat this step until the base is also completely coated in chocolate.

Place on a sheet of baking parchment, biscuit side down.

Sprinkle a few Maldon salt flakes on top then leave the chocolate to harden at room temperature.

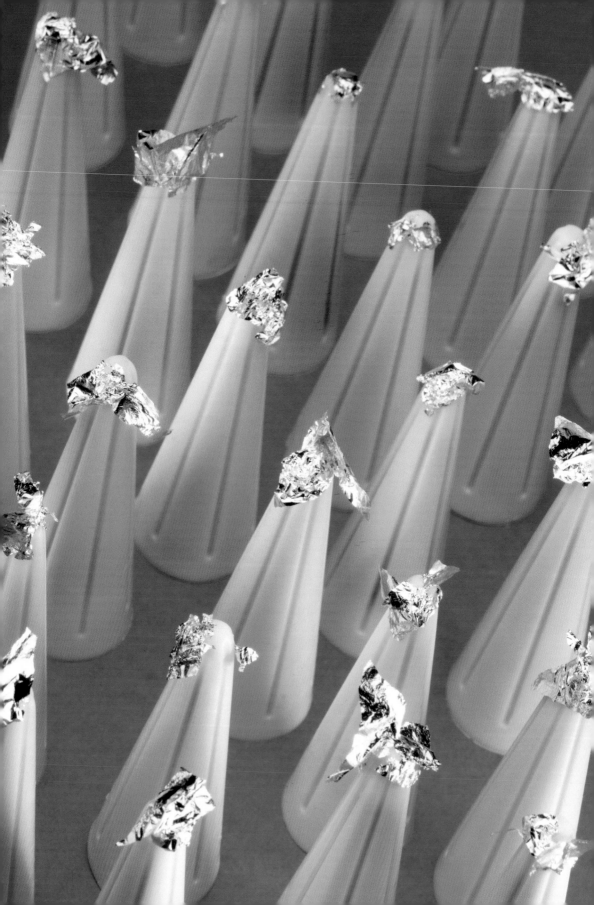

Passion fruit, lime and vodka

FOR 105 CHOCOLATES:
1 organic lime, 250g of frozen passion fruit purée, 10g of glucose, 300g of Costa Rica 64 dark chocolate, 50g of unsalted butter, 50g of vodka, edible silver leaf (optional)
For the mould:
Blanc Intense white chocolate
Mould cw HA 3666

Mould the shapes using tempered white chocolate (Moulding, p.249).

Rinse the lime in clear water. Grate a thin layer of peel. Add the peel into a mixture containing the lime juice and passion fruit purée.

Bring the entire mixture to the boil for 2 minutes then add the glucose. Gently mix.

Break the dark chocolate up into small pieces. Pour the hot mixture over the pieces.

Mix with a spatula until all the chocolate melts. Add in knobs of butter. Stir mixture until smooth.

Pour in the vodka, stirring all the while. Leave the fruity ganache produced to cool to 30°C.

Fill the moulds with the ganache, up to 1 mm from the top.

Leave the ganache to set in the refrigerator for 30 minutes.

Fill the remaining part of the moulds with tempered white chocolate.

Remove the pralines from the mould and garnish with a silver leaf if desired.

Bitter chocolate mousse

FOR 8 TO 10 PEOPLE:
10dl of fresh cream (40% fat content),
12 egg whites, 16g of icing sugar,
600g of Ecuador 71 dark chocolate,
1 pod of Madagascan vanilla, white spirit vinegar
(to remove fat from the bowl and beater)

Whisk 8dl of cream until semi-thick, then cover with plastic film and put in the refrigerator.

Use vinegar to remove the fat from the bowl and beater, then beat the egg whites and icing sugar until stiff. Put in the refrigerator.

Cut the chocolate into pieces and melt in a saucepan with the remaining 2dl of cream and the contents of the vanilla pod (previously scraped out using the tip of a knife). Do not exceed 50°C.

Mix to a smooth consistency. Leave to cool to 35°C.

Use a spatula to gently pour half the whipped cream into the chocolate mixture. Follow with the second half. Be careful! If you mix too much at once, the mixture will lose its light texture – if you mix too little, the chocolate won't spread through properly.

Mix the stiffly beaten egg whites into the chocolate mixture as gently as possible (to do this, use generous downward arm movements).

Use a piping bag (fitted with a wide nozzle to avoid pushing air out of the mixture) to fill glasses or a large glass bowl with the mixture.

Leave to set in the refrigerator. Cover with film. Check to see what else you have in the refrigerator, as the chocolate tends to rapidly absorb smells of other refrigerated food.

Dark chocolate ice cream

FOR 75CL OF ICE CREAM:
500g of full cream milk, 250g of fresh cream (40% fat content), 1 pod of Madagascan vanilla, 155g of Peru 64 dark chocolate, 7g of cornflour, 2cl of water, 7 egg yolks, 115g of caster sugar

The night before, mix the milk and cream together. Slit the vanilla pod in half and remove the contents using the tip of a knife. Add the emptied pod and its contents into the mixture. Bring to the boil. Remove the vanilla pod.

Cut the chocolate into pieces and melt into the mixture.

Dissolve the cornflour in a small amount of water. Add into the chocolate paste. Bring to the boil again. Whisk the egg yolks and sugar until the mixture takes on a yellowish, frothy ribbon texture. Pour 1/3 of the boiling chocolate mixture over this.

Gently stir with a spatula. Add this mixture to the rest of the chocolate, i.e. the remaining 2/3.

Mix together over a very low heat until you have a thick, smooth cream. Once the cream has thickened enough, transfer into a cold bowl to prevent any further cooking.

Leave to cool, cover with a plastic film and put in the refrigerator to settle. When the cream is ± 8°C, or after settling for 12 hours, swirl the mixture in an ice cream maker for at least 10 to 15 minutes.

Cocoa pod snow

FOR 300G OF SNOW:
4 fresh cocoa pods, 200g of water, juice of 1 lime

Cut the pods in half.

Remove the pulp and beans, then add water and a few drops of lime juice. Mix by hand until the pulp falls away from the beans.

Filter to separate the beans.

This "cocoa water" must be kept refrigerated and consumed within a short space of time.

Mixing it in a Thermos salad bowl with liquid nitrogen produces a truly aromatic sorbet.

To serve as granita-like flakes, freeze the cocoa water in a flat container. Roughly every 45 minutes, remove it from the freezer and scrape the surface with a fork. Repeat this process until you have your flakes.

The cocoa water can also be frozen in a Pacojet bowl. Before the sorbet stage, the Pacojet knife turns the frozen mixture into powder, in this case producing a snow effect.

"Mazat-lanica" Mexican oyster

FOR 90 CHOCOLATES:
60g of fresh oysters (juice and flesh),
90g of fresh cream (40% fat content),
180g of Blanc Intense white chocolate,
15g of Silver tequila, pearly silver colouring
powder DC102, sea salt, black pepper
For the mould:
Uganda 80 dark chocolate,
Blanc Intense white chocolate
For the oysters:
Mould cw 1158
For the pearls:
Mould cw 1495

Use a knife to open the oysters. Remove the oyster and keep the juice aside. Ensure that all fragments of shell are removed from the flesh and juice by filtering the juice.

Mix together the oyster flesh and juice. Bring the cream to the boil, adding the oysters in their juice. Break the white chocolate into pieces and cover with the mixture. Stir to an even consistency. Season with a dash of black pepper and if necessary a pinch of sea salt. The amount of salt depends on the type of oyster chosen; cupped oysters are typically more salty than flat oysters.

Add the tequila into the ganache and leave to cool. Pour a thin layer (2mm) of tempered chocolate fondant into the moulds chosen. Leave to crystallize in the refrigerator (Moulding, p.249).

To create the oyster pearls, fill half-sphere shape moulds with oyster ganache. Leave to set for 1 hour in the refrigerator, then position the half-spheres and cover in a thin layer of tempered white chocolate to produce attractive chocolate marbles. Leave to crystallize at room temperature.

Sprinkle the pearls with a touch of pearly silver colouring powder. Roll them around in a sieve to remove any excess powder.

Stick the pearl onto the oyster with a drop of tempered dark chocolate. Use a paper cone for this.

You can design your own moulds using a thermoforming machine, a sheet of fairly rigid plastic (PVC or acetate) and some oyster shells.

The moulds can also be created using a more traditional method. For this, place some oyster shells on a flat surface and cover with the plastic sheet. Using a heat gun (e.g. an electric paint remover), heat the plastic parts that are covering the shells.

Garlic confit in olive oil with Mexican coffee

Peel the garlic cloves and blanch in boiling water. Drain and absorb any remaining water. Put them into a small pan and cover with 1cm of olive oil.

Leave to simmer at 60°C for about 1 hour.

Remove from the heat and leave the garlic to cool in the olive oil.

Remove the cloves from the oil and gently absorb any excess oil.

Stick them onto brochettes then dip in tempered Costa Rica milk chocolate.

Make some coffee bean shavings and sprinkle over.

This recipe is a perfect example of food pairing. The coffee acts as an "aromatic bridge" between the garlic and chocolate, which on their own have little to offer each other.

FOR 20 CHOCOLATES:
20 fresh garlic cloves, extra virgin olive oil, 100g of Costa Rica 38 milk chocolate, 6g of Arabica coffee
Short sticks for brochettes (e.g. made of bamboo)

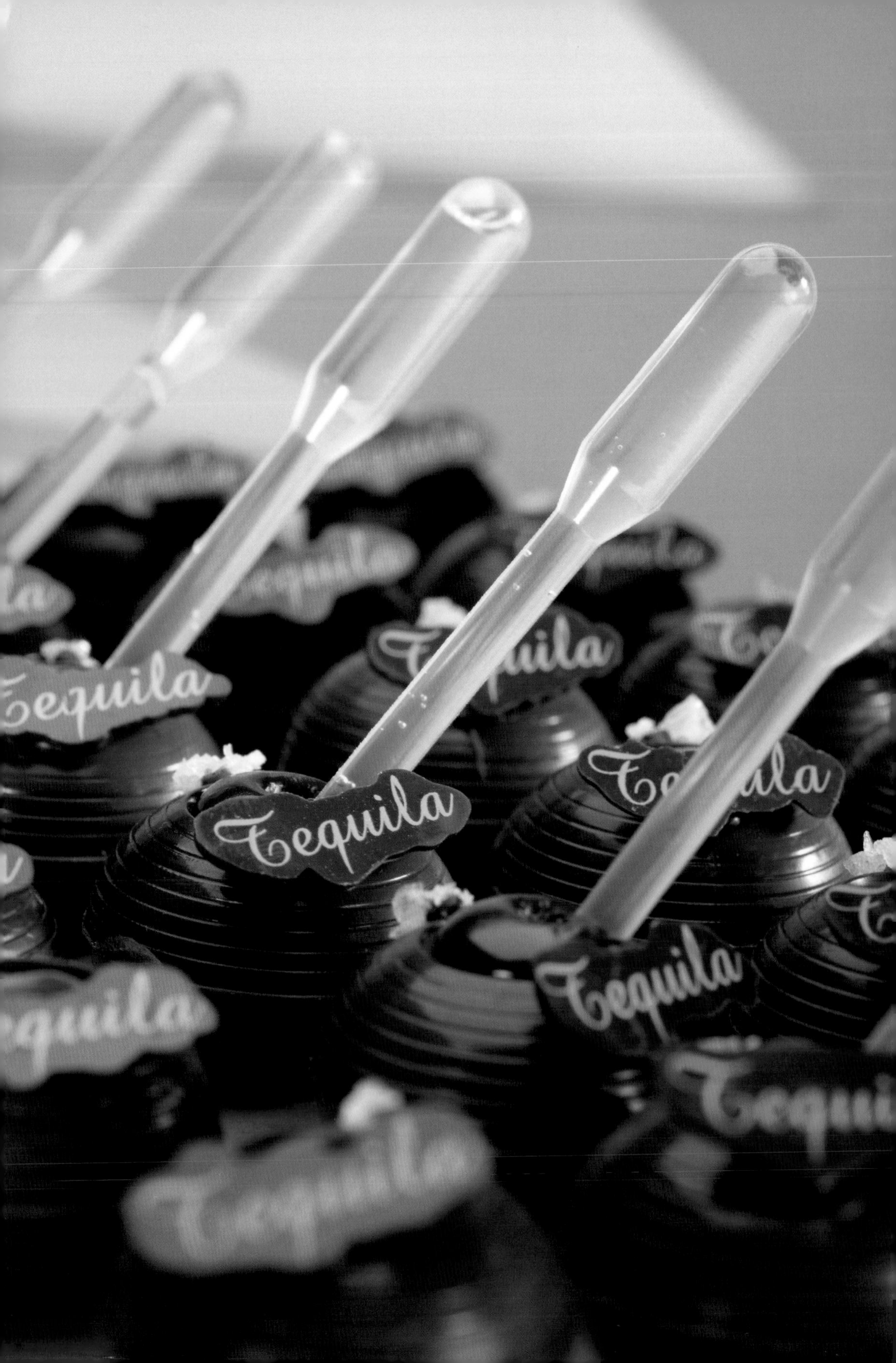
Tequila

Tequila Choc-tail

FOR 140 CHOCOLATES:
Peel and juice of 2 organic limes, 250g of fresh cream (40% fat content), 250g of glucose, 250g of Ecuador 71 dark chocolate, 125g of butter, Silver tequila, Maldon salt
For the mould:
Ecuador 71 dark chocolate
Mould Rondo CAO 0874
Customised tequila transfers
2ml pipettes

Use a piping bag to draw thin strips of tempered dark chocolate onto the tequila transfer designs. Leave to crystallize and put to the side.

Rinse the limes, wipe dry, then grate a thin layer of peel.

Squeeze the limes and briefly boil the juice with the peel.

Bring the cream to the boil and add the glucose. Cut the chocolate into small pieces and cover over with the cream mixture. Mix until all the chocolate melts.

Add the butter and cooled lime juice to this mixture. Put the ganache aside until it reaches 25 to 26°C.

Using a cone filled with tempered dark chocolate, stick a few Maldon salt crystals on one side of the mould.

Stick the tequila sign on the other side.

Using a syringe, fill the pipettes with tequila.

Fill the moulds using a piping bag containing ganache (still in liquid form). Place the pipettes into the ganache immediately. Leave to harden for 2 hours at room temperature.

Enjoy the choc-tail Mexican style: lick the salt, suck the tequila through the pipette, then devour the praline.

Mole poblano chocolate fondue

FOR 50 BALLS:
300g of poultry breast, 100g of ground pork, 1 egg, 140g of almond powder, 40g of sesame seeds, 1dl of extra virgin olive oil, 240g of Costa Rica 64 dark chocolate, 200g of fresh cream (40% fat content), 30g of mole paste (see Mole poblano, p.198), salt, pepper
Short sticks for brochettes (e.g. made of bamboo)

Using a dicing machine, finely mince the meat then add in the egg. Season with salt and pepper and gently mix.

Make small meat balls and roll through a mixture containing almond powder and sesame seeds. Heat olive oil in a pan and cook the meat balls medium rare.

Poke a brochette stick into each of the balls and keep warm.

Cut the chocolate into small pieces. Bring the cream to the boil then pour it over the pieces of chocolate. Mix until the chocolate melts. Add in the Mole Poblano paste. Stir again until the paste spreads right through the chocolate sauce.

Place a fondue dish on a dish-warmer and pour the sauce in.

Toss the hot poultry balls into the fondue.

Raspberry cocoa snuff

Weigh ingredients and mix together using a vegetable mill.
Filter the mixture produced using a fine sieve.
Inhale the chocolate powder using a Chocolate Shooter®.
After inhaling the powder, enjoy some raspberry sorbet, mousse, candy-floss, caramel, etc.
There you have it, a chocolate dessert, with no chocolate in sight!

50g of Peru cocoa powder, 1g of green mint powder extract, 3g of raspberry powder, 5g of red berries powder extract
Serve with:
raspberry ice cream

Basic Techniques

TEMPERING CHOCOLATE

Tempering gives a finished chocolate product its shine and smoothness, characteristic hardness, and long storage possibilities. The first step in the tempering process is to melt a piece of chocolate by heating it to about 45°C. Following this, let the chocolate cool to a final working temperature of: 31 to 32°C for dark chocolate, 29 to 30°C for milk chocolate, 28 to 29°C for white chocolate.
If an automatic tempering machine is not used, there are several other options available.

• TRADITIONAL METHOD
Heat the chocolate to 45°C until it completely melts – a bain-marie can be used for this. Pour 3/4 of the amount required onto cold marble. Use 2 palette knives to work the chocolate and cool it to 28°C. In a bowl, combine this chocolate with the remaining 1/4 (kept at 45°C). Carefully mix together with a spatula.

• IN THE MICROWAVE
Put 450g of chocolate in a plastic bowl and microwave on low. Stir from time to time until it reaches a temperature of 45°C. Beyond 50°C, the chocolate will burn. This can take 5 to 10 minutes, depending on the microwave used.
Add 50g of cold chocolate (previously cut into pieces and refrigerated). Mix well until all pieces melt.

• IN A THERMOMIX (for dark chocolate)
Cut the dark chocolate into pieces and put in a Thermomix. Mix at 37°C on level 6 until the chocolate melts.

USING CHOCOLATE WITH MOULDS

Pour tempered chocolate into all cavities of a mould (kept at room temperature).
Gently shake the mould for 5 seconds. This removes any air bubbles trapped in the mixture. Turn the mould over and tap with a spatula for 5 seconds such that the chocolate falls out of the mould. The aim is to obtain a fine layer of chocolate inside the mould.
Turn the mould over again head downwards and leave the chocolate to set for 5 to 10 minutes at room temperature (about 19°C).
Using a triangular palette knife, scrape away the excess chocolate which soon begins crystallizing at the top of the mould. Place the mould in a ventilated refrigerator, between 10 and 12°C. Leave chocolate to crystallize.
Keep an eye on the ambient moisture in the refrigerator and work area, as it should not exceed 60%. Also during this time, avoid cooking any products that give off steam.
At this stage, the shape is moulded and ready for filling. Once the content congeals, cover the shape in a fine layer of chocolate (kept at tempering temperature).
Leave the chocolate to crystallize for about 10 minutes at room temperature.
Remove the pralines from the mould.
Store in a dark place, the ideal conditions being 14°C and 60% hygrometry.

Basic Recipes

PUFF PASTRY

For a tray of 60cm x 40cm: 1kg of unsalted butter, 960g of flour, 270g of water, 2g of salt, flour (to make the rolled-out pastry)

The night before, make some puff pastry using the feuilletage inversé technique.
This requires two mixtures.
For the beurre manié, mix 1kg of butter with 480g of sieved flour.
For the détrempe, mix 480g of sieved flour with the water and salt. Roll out into a rectangle 40cm x 30cm.
Roll out the beurre manié between two sheets of baking parchment (60cm x 40cm).
Place the détrempe on one of the two halves of the beurre manié and fold the second half over top. Seal the edges using your fingers to prevent any air getting into the centre.
Refrigerate in baking parchment for 20 minutes to harden it up.
Remove the pastry from the refrigerator. Leave for 10 minutes to bring back to room temperature. Roll it out into a rectangle 1cm thick. To make this easier, sprinkle flour onto the pastry and work surface. Any excess flour should be brushed away during the folding steps to prevent the pastry from becoming too dry.
Fold the rectangle in 3 (1st time) by turning the pastry such that the opening (key) is on the right. To do this, fold the right third over the centre, then the left third also towards the centre, i.e. over the two others. Seal the edges and allow to rest in the refrigerator for 15 minutes.
Leave for 10 minutes to bring the pastry back to room temperature. Roll it out again into a rectangle 1cm thick and fold in 3 (2nd time), with the opening (key) towards the right. Seal the edges and allow to rest in the refrigerator for 15 minutes.
Leave for 10 minutes to bring back to room temperature. Roll it out again into a rectangle 1cm thick and fold in 3 (3rd time), with the opening (key) towards the right.
Allow the puff pastry to rest for 12 hours wrapped in baking parchment in a refrigerator.

Bring the pastry back to room temperature, roll out until 1cm thick, then fold in 3 (4th time) with the opening (key) towards the right.

Roll it into a strip 40cm x 60cm and 0.5cm thick.

Allow to rest in the refrigerator for 12 hours between two sheets of baking parchment. The puff pastry can be frozen for later use.

BISCUIT MIXTURE

For 600 g mixture : 125g of salted butter, 125g of icing sugar, 1 egg, 250g of flour, 50g of almond powder

Combine the butter and sugar in a bowl. Mix to an even consistency.

Add the egg (kept at room temperature) and mix again.

Pour in the flour and almond powder. Knead the mixture, but not excessively, to prevent it from becoming too hard. Wrap it in plastic film and leave to settle for 2 hours in the refrigerator.

Roll out the pastry mixture using a rolling pin. A sprinkling of flour will make this step easier. Brush away the flour once the pastry has been rolled out to a thickness of 0.5cm.

CARAMELISED COCONUT

For 100g: 15g of water, 45g of S2 caster sugar, 45g of grated coconut

Bring the water and sugar to the boil in a copper pan until you get a syrup. Continue cooking until it thickens. Add the coconut and mix with a spatula as it cooks, until the mixture turns a caramel colour.

Leave to cool on baking parchment. Pour the mixture through a coarse sieve.

Ingredients

The spices – even specifics such as achiote or annatto, Flor de Jamaica (Hibiscus sabdariffa) and dried peppers – are available from specialist grocers (www.ingredientsdumonde.be)
Agar-agar is usually available in Asian groceries or health food shops.
Food colourings are available from wholesale supliers of confectionery products.
Green mint extract and freeze-dried red fruits: www.sosa.cat
Cocoa powder: Belcolade Real Dutch Cocoapowder 22-24
Frozen cocoa pulp: produced by www.brasfrut.com.br
Frozen fruit purées: produced by Sicoly – www.sicoly.fr

Accessories

Moulds for chocolates: Most of the moulds used come from the catalogue of Chocolate World.
Drop-shaped pastry cutter: Chocolate World
Smoke pipe: Aladin Instant Smoke Pipe 100 % chef – www.100x100chef.com
Zester: Microplane®, Premium range – www.microplane.com
Personalized transfers can be made to order by IBC
Chocolate Shooter is exclusive to The Chocolate Line – www.chocolateshooter.com

Ingredients and Accessories

Belcolade
Industrielaan 16
I.Z. Zuid 3
9320 Erembodegem
Belgium
Tel: +32 53 83 96 00
www.belcolade.com
info@belcolade.com

Chocolate World
Lange Elzenstraat 123
2018 Antwerp
Belgium
Tel: +32 3 216 44 27
www.chocolateworld.be
info@chocolateworld.be

CNUDDE nv
Pontstraat 4
8791 Beveren-Leie
Belgium
Tel: +32 56 35 84 15
www.cnudde.com
cnudde@skynet.be

IBC Belgium
Waterven 7
8501 Kortrijk-Heule
Belgium
Tel: +32 56 22 39 87
www.ibcbelgium.com
ibc@ibcbelgium.com

PCB Création
7 rue de Suède
BP 67 - 67232 Benfeld
France
Tel: +33 3 88 587 333
www.pcb-creation.fr
pcb.creation@pcb-creation.fr

The Chocolate Museum

Choco-Story
Wijnzakstraat 2 (Sint-Jansplein)
8000 Brugge
Belgium
Tel/Fax: +32 50 61 22 37
www.choco-story.be
info@choco-story.be

The shops of Mathieu Brees

L'Amandine
Calle 5D Número 313   Entre 38 y 38A
Colonia Pensiones
97219 Mérida, Yucatán
Mexico
Tel/Fax: +52 999 920 58 69

Ki'Xocolatl
Santa Lucía, Calle 55   Número 513
Entre 60 y 62   Colonia Centro
97000 Mérida, Yucatán
Mexico
www.ki-xocolatl.com

Dominique Persoone

The Chocolate Line
Simon Stevinplein 19
8000 Brugge
Belgium
Tel: +32 50 34 10 90
www.thechocolateline.be
info@thechocolateline.be

Bibliography

AMADO Jorge. *Cacau*. Ariel Editora, 1933. 122 p.

BREADY James et al. *Les Mayas, Art et Civilisation*. Könemann, 2000. 480 p.

CHAPA Martha, SALAS Elsa, GONZÁLEZ DE LA VARA Martín. *Chocolate, Regalo del Edén*. Gobierno del Estado Tabasco, 2003. 156 p.

COATES Anthony G. et al. *Central America, A Natural and Cultural History*. Yale University Press, 1997. 277 p.

COE Michael D. *Les Maya, Mille ans de splendeur d'un people*. Armand Colin, 1987. 230 p.

COE Sophie D., COE Michael D. *The True History of Chocolate*. Thames & Hudson, 1996. 280 p.

FITCH Nancy. *The Conquest of Mexico, An annoted Bibliography* [online]. S.l. : s.n., s.d. http://faculty.fullerton.edu/nfitch/nehaha/conquestbib.htm.

GÓMEZ-POMPA Arturo et al. *The Sacred Cacao Groves of the Maya*. Latin American Antiquity, 1990, 1. Pp. 247-257.

LLOYD STEPHENS John, ACKERMAN Karl. *Incidents of Travel in Yucatan*. Smithsonian Institution Press, 1996. 286 p.

LOPEZ-BÁEZ Orlando, RAMÍREZ GONZÁLEZ Sandra Isabel. *La selección participativa y la conservación de la biodiversidad en los agroecosistemas*. In Agroecologia y Agricultura Orgánica en el Trópico. S.l.: s.n., s.d. Pp. 93-109.

LOWRY Malcolm. *Mezcal*. Plume, 1993. 111 p. (Degrés, 1)

MAES Freddy. *Le cacaoyer, La plante / Le cacao / Son passé et son avenir*. Tervuren: Africa Museum, 1996. 16 p. (Documentation, 1)

MAYORGA Francisco Mayorga, SÁNCHEZ Adriana Fabiola. *Recetario Indigena de Chiapas*. CONACULTA Culturas Populares è indígenas, 2000. 188 p. (Cocina Indigena y popular, 39)

McNEIL Cameron L. *Chocolate in Mesoamerica, A Cultural History of Cacao*. University Press of Florida, 2006. 542 p.

MOTAMAYOR J.C. et al. *Cacao domestication I: the origin of the cacao cultivated by the Mayas*. Heredity, 2002, 89. Pp. 380-386.

NORTON Marcy. *Sacred Gifts, Profane Pleasures, A History of Tobacco and Chocolate in the Atlantic World.* Cornell University Press, 2008, 352 p.

PÉREZ ROMERO José Alberto, s.n. (dir.). *Algunas Consideraciones sobre el Cacao en el Norte de la Península de Yucatán.* 73 p. Tesis professional, Ciencias Antropologicas, especialidad de Arqueologia. Merida, Yucatán, Mexico: Universidad Autónoma de Yucatán, 1988.

QUERO Julio César Javier. *Bebidas y Dulces tradicionales de Tabasco.* CONACULTA Culturas Populares è indígenas, 2000. 124 p. (Cocina Indigena y popular, 23)

SMITH Michael E. *Long-Distance Trade under the Aztec Empire, The archaeological evidence.* Ancient Mesoamerica, 1990, 1. Pp. 153-169.

TAIBO I Paco Ignacio. *El libro de todos los moles.* Ediciones B, 2003. 294 p.

VALLE Rafael Heliodoro. *Anales del Mole de Guajolote.* Puebla: Fundaciòn Amparo, 1991. 48 p.

VOGEL Susana. *TEOTIHUACAN, Histoire, Arts et Monuments.* Monclem Ediciones, 1995. 47 p.

YOUNG Allen M. *The Chocolate Tree, A Natural History of Cacao* (Revised and expanded edition). USA: Allen M. YOUNG, 2007. 219 p.

Cacao – The Roots of Chocolate
Dominique Persoone – Expedition in Mexico

Texts & Photographs:
Jean-Pierre Gabriel
Recipes:
Dominique Persoone
Editorial coordination:
Jean-Pierre Gabriel & Sophie Lepère
Design:
Jurgen Persijn
Translation:
David Bywell & Howard Curtis

Printed by Dereume in Belgium.

© 2008 Editions Françoise Blouard, Jean-Pierre Gabriel (Texts & Photographs)
& Dominique Persoone (Recipes)

D/2008/10612/12

ISBN 978-2-87510-006-1
EAN 9782875100061

www.francoiseblouard.com
www.belcolade.com
www.thechocolateline.be